# About the author

Margaret Beaver is a sixteen-year-old high school junior who began writing at the age of eight and has since partnered that with interests in photography, illustration, and tutoring fellow classmates in the algorithms of literature. She currently resides in her hometown of Plano, Texas, and can be found browsing in any local bookstore. *inkwells.* is her first publication, a poetry collection which was written at the age of fourteen.

Follow her literary ventures on Instagram @iammargaretbeaver, and for book recommendations, visit @margaretwritesonwalls.

# inkwells.
a poetry collection

# MARGARET BEAVER

---

## inkwells.
### a poetry collection

Vanguard Press

VANGUARD PAPERBACK

© Copyright 2022
**Margaret Beaver**

The right of Margaret Beaver to be identified as author of
this work has been asserted by her in accordance with the
Copyright, Designs and Patents Act 1988.

A CIP catalogue record for this title is
available from the British Library.

ISBN 978 1 80016 380 5

*Vanguard Press is an imprint of
Pegasus Elliot MacKenzie Publishers Ltd.*
www.pegasuspublishers.com

First Published in 2022

**Vanguard Press
Sheraton House Castle Park
Cambridge England**

Printed & Bound in Great Britain

## *dedication*

i dedicate this collection to fate, for it gifted me my mentors, each of whom i will forever treasure: my fifth-grade homeroom teacher, mrs. probst; my sixth-grade language arts teacher, mrs. yake; and my ninth grade english teacher, mrs. dunn.

and, of course, to my beloved parents—the reasons i am more than a small, undetectable piece in this whole wide world.

and, to sam. you made the list, congratulations.

## a message from the author

*inkwells.* is the product of the worst mental health relapse of my life thus far, which was caused by the fact that I'd been doing extraordinarily well in ignoring and neglecting my symptoms when my body and mind were clearly warring, and I opted to remain the nonchalant referee.

For people both battling and not battling with mental health disorders of any degree, there is specific subject matter and blunt language used at frequent intervals throughout the work which may appear disturbing, as the collective and comprehensive themes of *inkwells.* are mental health, self-harm and thoughts of suicide. This message will be the *only* trigger warning incorporated so as to not wrongfully gauge which poems may or may not be triggering according to an individual reader, and to not disrupt the flow of the work. I urge any and all readers to confront any negative feelings which may, understandably, be triggered due to the dark themes, and discontinue reading this work should the subject matter become too impactful.

*inkwells.* is my chronicling of the authentic and realistic notions which I created as a sort of self-medication to abstain from the self-destructive urges I was experiencing. Under no circumstances should any reader compromise their mental health to analyze or endure mine.

I wish you all the best during your mental health journey, and I remind you confidently and honestly that recovery is possible. Please stick around to see it.

Be safe and well,
Margaret Beaver

# Contents

Sad boy ........................................................ 13

bridges ........................................................ 15

burning ........................................................ 22

Fine Line ...................................................... 25

fishbowl ....................................................... 30

Girl of Thunder .............................................. 32

home ........................................................... 36

I am an arborist ............................................. 40

I Dare Me ..................................................... 45

Just a Little More Me ...................................... 50

Love is to Burn ............................................. 56

poets dream .................................................. 59

Questions & Regrets ....................................... 63

Wallflower .................................................... 66

orchid .......................................................... 70

half girl ....................................................... 76

There Will Be Peace ....................................... 80

me & my ghost .............................................. 86

childhood revival ........................................... 89

Die in dignity ................................................ 95

landing ........................................................ 99

sad // healed ............................................... 104

reminders .................................................... 109

The visionary ............................................... 112

looking glass ................................................ 116

it doesn't have to make sense ........................... 121

my crown is made of warning signs .................... 126

Avenue...................................................................... 132

I love you................................................................ 136

we are infinite ........................................................ 141

Sister Feline............................................................ 147

chameleon............................................................... 151

On the bayou .......................................................... 159

Know our names..................................................... 164

Parental Guidance.................................................. 168

meg.......................................................................... 174

inkwells .................................................................. 178

Mom (bonus piece)................................................. 183

feeling suicidal?...................................................... 188

# *Sad boy*

Strung out in the back of a black car,
Frequent haze dawns on me from afar
And I know I've been here before

Blare loud an atom bomb in this agony;
I need to find a place, of release
If only I could see the sky

Pools of red flake down from the ache
I have to find a way, out of this place
But I know this is only a single feather in the wing of time

But here we lie, strung out in this black car
I fist your shirt, to find your heart
But I'm beyond these untimely faults

Boy, it sure is a sad life,
Begging a sad boy to stay and have a sad time

Maybe it's the thought that counts?

Side to side, we trace our clues
But it all comes circling back to you
Is there something I can do?

But we only ask when it's too late
When we're too far gone, in this abstract place
If only you could see the sky

I wish you could see the sky


*Topical Winner of the "Inside of Me" 2019/2020 Live Poets Society*
*Publication.*

*I wish you could see the sky.*

## *bridges*

I've been tired a lot these days
Don't take it the wrong way
I have never been the one to have too terribly much to say
I quite like silences too
I wish they'd prolong for a while
And not be rashly interrupted by someone who just can't stand them

Truthfully, I think if you hate silences
We're better off not being friends
I don't talk a lot
But I make up for it with my thoughts
I think too much
Too much, in fact, for my own good
I play these games with myself
See how long I can go without getting help
My brain taunts me with images I'm at peace with
Convinces me to give it one more good look
See if anything is obscured
Anything I can dwell on to make myself hurt

I've been angry a lot these days
I'm not one who fakes being okay
Or at least I don't think so
I may just suppress it a little

If I hide I don't mean to
No harm I'd ever do to you
Would ever be intentional
Sometimes I just get hasty

Hurt myself day in, day out
I can't stop myself when I'm full of doubt
Truthfully, I don't even know what I'm doubting
But I'm doubting something

I can sit in silences fine
But when I'm in the presence of someone else's decline
You can't just expect me to sit and waste when I can help you
Honestly, I don't even know how
Talk myself down from anything I could offer you
But I just want you to know that I think about caring for you a lot

But sometimes thinking isn't enough
Sometimes I think I'm the only one
And then I'm reminded that millions of us are silent
I wish I could tell you it's comforting
Knowing someone else out there is struggling
But it just makes me hate me that I can't do anything to solve it

I've been sad a lot these days
Perpetual panic seems to push people away
Or maybe that's just me
Doing what I seem to do best

Ruining everything with a second guess
Come over, try to get me out of my head
Maybe I'm too attached to the attention
Too infatuated with the occupation
Of someone who knows they can do better

What even is "better"?

I got something I gotta get off my chest
I'm just so tired of never living outside of my head
It takes nothing in me to push people away
Convince myself I deserve it; there's no other way
I wish I could explain
How pain is just so
Cold

I don't know how to explain it but it's cold

And it's numb
And it's scorching hot
And it's breathing fire
And it's false desire
And it's faking laughter
And it's walking in circles
And it's always feeling mean
And it's like everything's your fault, even the little tiny things
And it's nothing but a sad, empty road

I guess I've always liked
The long way home

I've been anxious a lot these days
I've used that word a lot to say
That I'm terrified of forever being taken for granted
Maybe that's why I've turned so mean
I can't care about anything
I'm too filled up caring about things I know don't even matter

It's like a phone out of storage
Get the alerts but you always ignore them
It's just simply deleting the games you don't even play
But it's the effort it takes
You don't want to deal with it anyway
You click "remind me later"
But later, it just never comes

The worst part is being self-aware
I know exactly how I'm draining; I'm not impaired
And I can't talk about it because I know I'll drain you too
I just don't want to hurt you
Or anything else, if I can stop myself
I'm the living proof I'm a killing machine
I just can't do it; I understand if you leave
But I hope that you leave with love

It's all I ever wanted

I'm so tired of trying to keep everyone afloat
Worry so much about everyone else
I have no room for me
I don't even care to see
Why I've done it

Wonder so much about how to make it stop
Don't even think about how I broke the parts
Maybe I should take it back to when it all started
Ten years old and two smiles away
From officially breaking my face
So young and oblivious
Sinking into the abyss
If I'd known, would I have stopped it?

Like an actress with an addiction
Play broken people so long you turn into them
But you stick to the script
Go home and reminisce
Were you ever happy?

I'm not interested in my excuses
I need to know why I'm doing this
When I decided I was low enough to sink
And not even mean a thing
A tortured soul
A victim out of control
Did it ever mean anything?

I've been bitter a lot these days
Too tired to love and hate
It's just antipathy and disinterest
Or maybe, if you're lucky, I'll scrape up some Nothing At All

You think it hurts you?
Say it like it doesn't hurt me too
I'm the one who left
I'm the one with the debts
I try to come back
But I stop when it gets bad
Wonder why I even care at all

All the blood stains and running
All the wine spills and hunting
Wonder how I can forgive myself
For always succumbing

Truth be told, it's not about you
You can't fix me the way you want to
Trust me, I've tried, a black and blue eye
Accidentally stay up till four
Nothing I want to do any more
You lose motivation
Dangle on the temptation
I'm not sure what I'm fighting for
Or if I'm fighting at all

It's not that I'm gone
I'm just harder to see
Buried beneath the numbness and uncertainty
I'll resurface; I know I will
But for the time being
This is an awfully bitter pill
To sit and to wait
For the fake sentiment to take place
Tell me how you care
And I'll tell you how I don't

It's a polished regret
And a bit of whiskey

I never drank
Somehow I'm tipsy
I could treat me better if I really wanted to
Guess I wouldn't know the difference

Stare out the window at the Golden Gate
San Francisco never felt the same
I'm not sure I've met my bridges yet;
I'll know when I burn them down

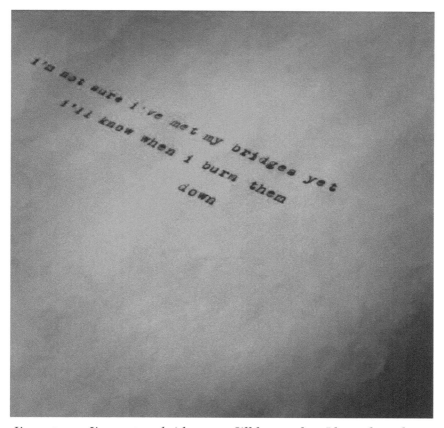

*I'm not sure I've met my bridges yet; I'll know when I burn them down.*

# *burning*

Eyes burning, grab my hand
Giving me a second chance
Shed some dark to shed some light
I feel it coming; grab a knife

On the cusp of my regrets
Driving a nightmare, I digress
Say I'm hopeless, expect reactions from the press
Over-exaggerate my place in people's lives
Always walking the edge of this divide
Say I'm helpless, why can't you help me?
Feel like loving myself is such a felony
Constant repetition, all these epiphanies
Think my normal thoughts are something so extraordinary

Self-esteem's a bit confused
Think I'm royalty, a tad abused
As low as they come, I can't refute
Can't tell which thoughts are actually true
Despicable, deserves to be used
How am I better than those I've accused?

Hold my hand, I'm sinking
My binding is unraveling
Need to feel warm without getting any closer
Isn't self-love just self-hatred's exposure?

But it's my fault; I know it's true
It's well deserved, what I've gone through
My selfishness finally sank in
Wonder when I'll laugh again
Without it feeling like an accident

Say you're here, but I can't feel you

Say you care, yet I resist you
Give me peace, and then I fall through
Every circumstance is impromptu
Why won't I let me breathe

Stay away, this is burning
Anger's selected to be never-ending
Danger is impending
Or at least the feeling

Want to scream but I stay speechless
Can't ask for help; it's only weakness
Wonder of a life living guiltless
Maybe I should work harder on forgiveness

Trade my bliss for my own safety
But is it safety if it destroys me?
Everything, collapsing
Watch my bridges burning
How underwhelming it is to be overwhelmed

Let me go, I'm reaching
For something I'm not seeing
I would take the shortcut home
But the house is burning

*Danger is impending, or at least the feeling.*

# Fine Line

Romeo and Juliet taught us
Main characters were never safe from death
Is it the mistakes we fear,
Or the reactions?
We wade in our despair, dwelling on it,
Don't we?

I would say I'm sorry for you
But you hear that a lot, don't you?
Wear those sad eyes like a string of diamonds
Wonder how long it'll take you to realize how good you had it
Wish we treasured the innocence before intelligence befell us

Does asking strangers for answers help you?
Do you still blame yourself when things fall through?
I hope you realize now,
You don't hate the summer
Wish you never settled for the cold of winter
You wish you never tried so hard to become her
Or perhaps that's just my dreams; you know how they scatter

Did you lose that longing,
Or are you still walking that trail of warning?
Did you ever kill the yearnings,
The cravings you could never fill?
How you used to drain your water
Didn't your mother ever teach you to pour from the saucer?

I love not you but the idea
How far you grew when I needed you near
I guess it was harder for you to love than to disappear
Now naïve I was to strip your exterior

I hope you've learned you don't fear attraction

You're only tired of being someone's distraction
I hope you've traced the clues of your destruction
How it all circles back to you

How easily you broke beneath the weight of the earth
How many times I refuted, said it wasn't what you deserved
I wish you would've let me clean the dirt out of your laundry
I wish you wouldn't have dug so many holes around yourself, empty
That's what you were
Nothing I could've deterred

How many times you'd yell when I got scared for you
Often, it seemed, you'd forgotten I had feelings too
And these stitches don't stick with just scissors and glue
And not in a blur did I see what was coming
How precisely the words on my lips, they were forming

All of your falling, was it ever exhausting?
You never asked once, entertained with comparing
How easy lies come once you're acquainted
But it was not red but blood with which you painted

I would say I'm sorry for you
But you hear that a lot, don't you?
Your baggage lines the hall of my building
Put me under the gun when my endurance was thinning

We traded our souls for some color
You offered your red, felt more like a collar
Some nights we'd eye the sunsets
How come you only liked the thunder?
But we never could grow together,
Could we?

Project your anger into that starless blue
Me or the sky, sometimes I'd confuse

Sometimes I'd like to believe you tried
But you tried less at love and more to hide
But love has a deadline
And we've overstayed this fine line
I said to steady the ladder as I climbed down from here
But you never did listen,
Did you?

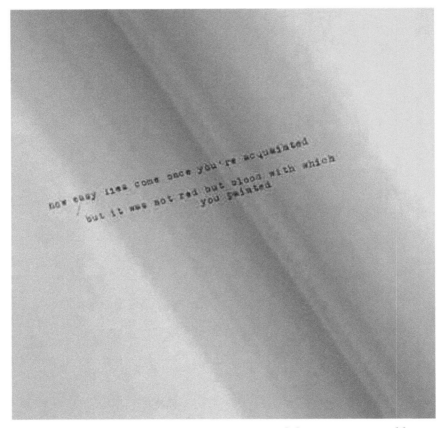

*How easy lies come once you're acquainted, but it was not red but
blood with which you painted.*

*Did you ever kill the yearnings, the cravings you could never fill?*

# *fishbowl*

I kidnapped logical me
Manic me took her to her fate unforeseen
Ever so calm as it all sets in
The emergency lights and the caving in
My obligations press the glass
Everything I've ever wanted; I watch it pass
Schoolwork knocks and emails pile
All the wrong words unify in my denial
Why is it I love everything I can lose?
Watch my castle in the sky shatter with the fate I didn't choose
Mediocre burdens entangle as they circle the sky
All my liabilities shaken, try to tunnel under disguised
Talk myself down from anything I can offer myself
To do or to not, I'll regret both nevertheless
Float in the flow of my indiscretions unforgiven
Watch in a dead paralysis of my forelife forever rewritten
If anything, I've learned, not a problem worrying solves
You watch the pool dry and I'll watch me dissolve
Come on over, get me out of my head
Mama, I'm trapped in my fishbowl again

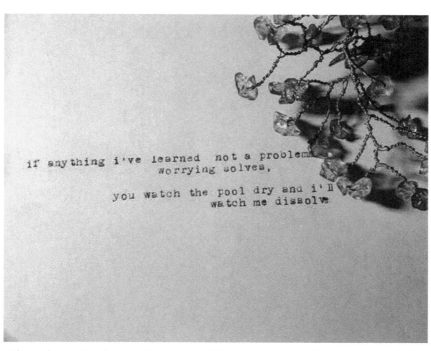

*If anything I've learned, not a problem worrying solves; you watch the pool dry and I'll watch me dissolve.*

# Girl of Thunder

You often wander my lonely mind, did you know?
An exhausted plain willing to entertain a sorry soul
I fear this is the last time you'll see my brain alive
Self-destruct on my own dime

What a pity to live a life so full of love
And deprive yourself of all of it, all at once
Who made you believe you were so undeserving?
Who made you decide your presence was so unnerving?
I bet it was you

Doing what I do best
Talking over tightropes, these words are thin
It's hard to balance when it all caves in
Sometimes bonds just disappear
I wonder where they go
Because it's not here
Who made me feel so disastrous?
Who made me think I was a gaping tide of ashes?
I bet it was you

Or maybe I'm just selfish
For not letting you take me down
Dancing with our hands tied, joined at the hip
Your gloom met my doom on the night that we slipped
Our broken legs chased a perfection we couldn't find in each other
Made one fatal mistake, choosing the girl who reflected clear sky
But all she knew was thunder

She lived a life treading water
Never knew more time than a single feather
Wishing you had never bothered
Wondered what you gained from her misdirection
Bullet holes of indiscretions

Surfing waves of self-deception
A hurricane's bloodthirst met a cabinet of wonder
That was the night she became the thunder

Drew the line between deceit and truth
To cut her flowers, you left her roots
And with her roots, she will grow again
on the tide, a gracious blue
Her worst fear: becoming an impoverished story
With prosperous reviews

Ever feel like you're running out of time?
Fleeing through a jungle as your eyes are going blind
To feel so completely helpless, at the hands that bleed red
It's a pity, how the worst ones always live in your head
But you shall rest easy, she is nobody else's but her own
But a moment's time, and she is yours
To be so cold the garden never grew
That is how it felt being loved by you

She refuses to promise love,
For it is her fate
And fates, you see,
Are seldom promised
And how ironic it be, that the saddest one was her smile
To swim so freely in this fountain of unbreakable denial

So tell my doubts I'm coming home
I'll wipe my feet off at the door
To live the life as pain was born
My girl of thunder rests here no more

*Her worst fear: becoming an impoverished story with prosperous reviews.*

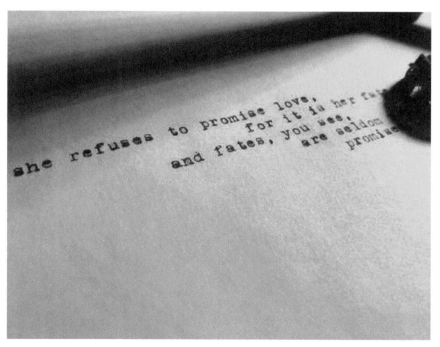

*She refuses to promise love, for it is her fate. And fates, you see, are seldom promised.*

# *home*

I'm gonna call my mother
It's been a while since it's felt like home
Been a while since the nostalgia flowed
Storm passed, looked green outside
Reminded me of an old friend
Wonder if she still looks on the bright side

Brother's growing up fast
Or maybe that's just me being unaware, floundering around in the past
Can still hear his boy voice on his old voicemail
How fast he ran to finally get somewhere
I hope he knows I get it now

Could use a little rainbow these days
No one knows how hard it was for me to drop off
Living off some deranged clock
Always telling me I'm running out of time
I've always been the sentimental type
To feel so behind, being ahead
It's a color I couldn't see but now I've found
Wish I knew then what I know now

I don't think I'm going to live in regret
Wishing I could have done this, could have tried that
Mom worries I've been missing out on life
To watch your daughter drive the edge of the knife
Perpetually pondering this crazed design
To drown in love yet thirst for none

Dad's got it going for him now
Forging his own path
Hope he's making himself proud
I hope he likes what it feels like
Toss around dysfunction like a family heirloom

Share the same mind, you and I, unify in our adjoined doom
The emotional type, think he's where I get it from
Circumstance can make you stop but it's you who decides when you're done
I'm learning how to show myself love and give you some
Have to wade in the tide until the damage comes undone
Just bear with me, the transformation has nearly begun

Been a few years since I've talked to someone my age
Hard to find things in common when the mindset is out of place
Terrified I'll get wrapped up in things I shouldn't
Just how easy it is to snap in the winds of change
Perceive yourself so weakly, you'll never know strength

Yes, Mom, I'm on the road
A few more miles, almost home
Gonna take a pit stop on the way
Yes, I promise I won't be late
I love you too, I'll see you soon
The timing isn't bad for you?
Okay, just making sure

Press the pedal, burning gas
Eye the street signs, watch time pass
Motion slows and tears drip lightly
Time nothing but a flimsy feather
Clammy fingers, standing close
Eye to eye, not face to face
Press the glass, a silent embrace
I watch you sift through the clouded headspace

Mom, I'm home, pick up the phone
I'm here now, won't let you go alone
Just watch my imprint linger slowly
I'll make this feel like home

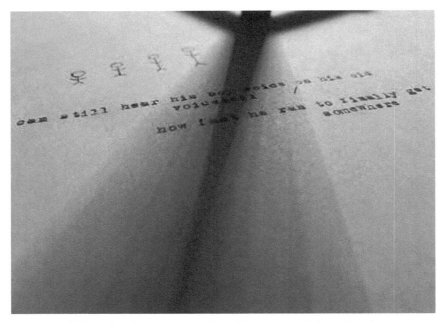

*Can still hear his boy voice on his old voicemail, how fast he ran to finally get somewhere.*

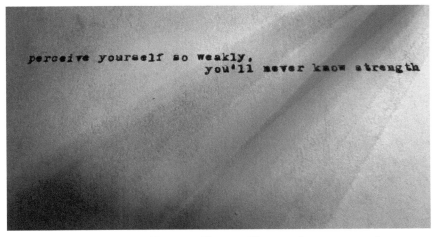

*Perceive yourself so weakly, you'll never know strength.*

## I am an arborist

I guess I held on too tight to something that wasn't even there
But that's just what I do
The kind of person that I am
Kindness with no expectation of reciprocation
And it shatters you

It's not that you're gone
Maybe you're just harder to see
Maybe if I look around
I'll still find some form of peace

But that's a fragile hope
Waiting for a wrecked ship to return whole
But that's just what I do
The kind of person that I am
Holding on too tight to things I can't accept

I squint down at the sea
Searching for the parts
If anything floods in, would you let me know?
I wait around all day
Sifting through the sand
If anything drifts by, would you let me know?

And it's an exhausting thing
But trickery is peace
It's not that I can't exist without you
But I only ever lived with you

Sure, it's a fragile hope
Waiting for the world
To return what's left of me
So I can put back all the parts
But it's my passion to pursue

One I hope that follows through
So I wait around for days
Luckily, I have enough adrenaline to exhaust

You say we're big enough people to forgive
But I can't shake that forgiving is giving up
And if anything, I know
We are a tree that rarely grows
Do you really want to cut us down?

I am not a doctor
It is not my right to fix other people
Instead, I am an arborist
And you cut down my tree
You say we're big enough people to forgive
But how can I forgive
The slaughter of a rare flourishment
And all I saw in me?

Maybe I'm not kind
Maybe it's a curse
Maybe it was a pure illusion, a mass deception
You injected in me first

Or maybe it's my fault
Something that I did
Didn't you love me as much as the devil loved playing with our heads?

Maybe it's a fragile hope
Waiting for a wrecked ship to return whole
But that's just what I do
The kind of person that I am
Holding on too tight to things I never truly had

Or maybe I did have you
And you just didn't know what to do

With such a force rested on your feeble shoulders
And maybe I crushed you
With everything I was
Wait until I learn just how much I can love myself

And with love I can say
That you upped and walked away
From what crushed you
And what told me
That I was too much to take

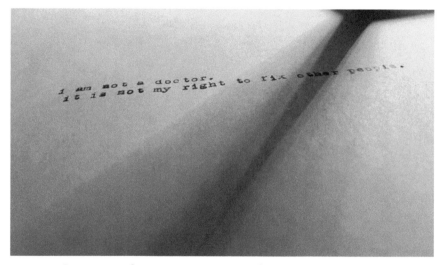

*I am not a doctor. It is not my right to fix other people.*

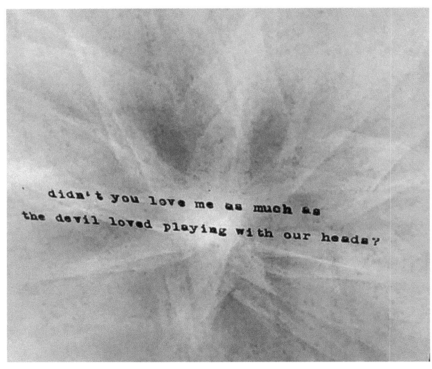

*Didn't you love me as much as the devil loved playing with our heads?*

# I Dare Me

Standing in the dark, pacing my thoughts steady
Compulsive isolation never stops me from obsessing
It's ironic, really; how emptiness feels so heavy

I've been holding back tears, overwhelmed with my fears
Numbness never hurt so badly
Now I'm watching the cars roll down the boulevard
Wish there were something that could stop me

My hair is framing my face, I'm ignoring the chafe
Squinting in the sun
I'm way too far south, think I need a new map
Not ready to come back

I've been counting to ten, been surrounded with dread
Because of something I said
Funny how something so small, so meager and poor, can blare so
loudly
Wasn't even my fault; if I could just stand up and talk
It could all be forgiven

I've been sweating a lot, clammy fingers so stiff
Never so tempting, the whirling abyss
Wish I would sink and not swim
But I'm already drowning, without even touching the water

I've been hostile a lot, too bitter now to give thought
To how I could be myself
So hellbent on the idea, that I just need something real
And everything would reappear

So deathly afraid of change, so terrified of staying the same
Wish these memories, I could erase
But I've been lying in bed, thinking about what you said

How I feed it with my dread
How dare you give me advice, when you live a life
Never having to think twice
About speaking your mind or raising your hand, giving things a second chance
When nothing ever goes to plan

I've been living a life, just trying to get by
With these swollen, dead eyes
I've never had a problem telling the truth, until the truth was stark and rude
Not a thing could quench this thirst for solitude

I've been selfish a lot, cutting people off at all costs
I just want to be alone
But then the questions come again, you know how they always fill your head
Something I'll have to get used to

But I'm afraid of change
How can I act shocked when things stay the same?
I've had it with me, just want to be free
And if not free, then at least away
From all the misery and pain
I dare me to go home

I dare me to go home and for once not be alone
Stare in the mirror, turn off my phone
Realize the girl inside, she has quite the diamond mind
If only I'd known

Go sit out on the porch, go look out at the cold
Realize I've always been bold, telling it like it is
How could I have missed it?

Sure, I do what I'm told, try to fit in the mold

All my doubts, I attempt to withhold
I dare me to understand
There's nothing wrong with being bland
On the surface
And when I feel invalidly, remember that it's always me
Telling myself the level of dysfunction I'm required to meet

I dare me to light a candle at midnight
Stare into the stars through the candlelight
Not be frightened of the flame
And last a whole day without feeling guilty
Paralyzingly empty, for the truth that I say

I've been angry a lot; in fact, I pride myself on it
My little unhealthy attainment
I guess no one would have thought
That innocent girl, soft-spoken heart
Would endure so much grief and loss

And when you stare up at the sky
And see the child with brown eyes,
You should come knocking
I quite like company, you see
A new revelation, unforeseen
I'm sorry if it's startling

And when you stare up at the sky
And see that brilliant red light,
You should know, you've met my partner in crime
My diamond flame of the night,
He grew into his fire
And he's doing just fine keeping the day sky alight

We're twin lovers of the sky,
But I soon found daytime hurt my eyes
I longed for the fog of the night

But he worried I'd be alone
Packed his bags and moved close
We chat at night sometimes

I dare me to go home, start experiencing on my own
I think I owe it to my soul
I'm capable of more than I know
Starlight shatters me in this hold
Surely I know where I can go

And all at once, I peel myself from the night
Try to hide the fear in my eyes
Should I bother with goodbye?

Toes land in the fresh-mown lawn
To say farewell, should I wait till dawn?
Get the markers out of the drawer now
Surely a smile can be drawn

Nighttime never lived so darkly
Poltergeists, the prey behind me
I wonder if he's lonely

I dare me to light a candle at midnight
Stare into the stars through the candlelight
Not be frightened of the flame
And last a whole day without feeling guilty
Paralyzingly empty, for the truth that I say

But I'd be worried he'd be lonely
Gaze at his fire glowing slowly
We chat at night sometimes

*It's ironic, really; how emptiness feels so heavy.*

## Just a Little More Me

Was raised religious
But I wish that I weren't
Having something to believe in
Gave me a reason not to believe in myself

I stopped about twelve
When I fell into myself
Realized I liked the universe more than any god
Does that make me a devil?
Don't really care because my cup is still half full

Diagnosed at fourteen but felt it from ten
These poisonous whirlwinds just stuck in my head
I wouldn't say I struggle because I'm really quite good at it
Suppress it and drown it just like any addict
But my addictions aren't tangible solids and liquids
More like mental misery and self-loathing and feeling like I deserve it

I'd see a lightning-struck tent in the middle of the woods
Say, not much of a shelter for not much of a girl
I'd rest there all night with beetles festering and twigs pricking my skin
And I'd wake up and I'd do it all over again

Got me some liquid in a measuring cup
Felt guilty for still bargaining with death to give up
Was offered some pills but was too scared to take them
Didn't want to choke and die without my will written

I cut my hair and closed all my blinds
Played metal music from nine to five
I always thought it was too loud
And I still do
But sometimes the loud things are the only ones that get through

Once a song told me I can't be saved from the sins I've ignored
I stayed up till dawn writing poetry as it poured
And thought, do sins still exist, if I don't believe?
I guess when I stopped I was granted a "get out of jail free" card
Maybe that's why I could finally breathe

I tried to pray one day but didn't know what to say
It feels like I was betraying a personal commitment to this day
To shut out and lock out things I can do without
Once I start adding things to the list I get overwhelmed with self-doubt

Sure, it's true, that I shut out positive things to lessen my load
But my life is mine and I learned that all on my own
I don't want the influence of a god that seems to persist
And I don't need religion to know the devil exists

I'm sorry for guilting you when I push you away
When my depressive episodes take me to a different state
Yell at you for never asking if I'm okay
But we both know I wouldn't reply, whether you checked on me or not
Probably just think you were pitying me for everything I'm not
More energetic in the beginning, as they all are
But my constant negativity soaked in and you held me afar
But it's hard communicating with someone who went through the same situation
And still came out okay

Doing well at school now, you got your friends
I used to be jealous but now I'm content
Even then my jealousy was quiet because I knew it was irrational
A general response of mine to any emotion at all
Truthfully, I'm happy you're doing so well
And I'm always here for when you're going through hell
Not much I can do from a thousand miles away
But maybe I can put your mind in a different place

But helping you reminds me how I give and I give
And guilt myself for having no expectation of receiving the same
Kindness to a fault only teaches you one thing
And that's how kindness is white lies of the ache in your back
Of bending over backwards and getting up fast
Before anyone sees that you almost broke
Being trampled on at the doorsteps of the people you know

And in spite of this knowledge I've collected about myself,
I attempt to retaliate and climb out of the well
But rebellion just translates to lashing out at you
Telling you how it hurts from my perspective of everything I've gone through
Maybe I really am a manic depressive with a chip on my shoulder
But that chip is the devil and he never grows older
Young and alive with every lie he feeds me, an anger to never dissolve in the pain of this misery
Am I really doing more, though?
Am I really all I say?
Maybe I deserve it
Maybe I'm self-centered
That's the pain talking now, and I'm sorry that I shut down when it all gets too loud

I tried to watch a movie the other day
To spark some emotions amidst the decay
It worked in reminding me of how I'll never grow closer
In any relationship, in any point in time
I'll never be capable of getting out of my mind
I cried for two hours, red in the face
It felt good to release but was sent to a different place
Dizzy for three days in the height of my mania
Played a game with myself to see how fast I could fold the laundry
So I had a reason for my frantic breaths when faced with this poor quandary

And I know
That one day
It's all going to be different
Wear yellow on weekends and put red in my cheeks
Take some pictures of me in my foggy desk mirror
Maybe if I wear happy colors I won't be so sad
Maybe if I wear some turquoise I won't look half bad
Begged my mom for barrettes on Tuesday, should get them by Friday
I'll wear them to the living room and dance in the refrigerator light

Because I know that I'll fight it for the rest of my life
But I'll make sure I'm having one hell of a time
Wake you up at two to take me to the doctor
And I won't feel guilty for asking for food after
I'll tell you my dreams and you'll say they're insane
Then you'll say that makes sense coming from someone who circles the drain

And maybe I'll dye my hair blue and put on winged eyeliner
Maybe I'll borrow some of your precious designer
I don't have a taste for it, but I don't really care
I'll make sure to compliment myself, a silent prayer

I'll draw smiley faces on balloons, and I'll hug my cat
Tell him to stop eating plastic or I'll take him right back
Put on my glasses without worrying
About looking in the mirror and hating what I see

And I'll blare Taylor Swift while I'm in the shower
Shuffle between *Getaway Car* and *Wonderland* for hours
And I'll convince myself that this isn't a dream
That my bazillion milliliters of Prozac are actually doing their thing
Because that's what I want
And that's what I deserve
Just a little more me

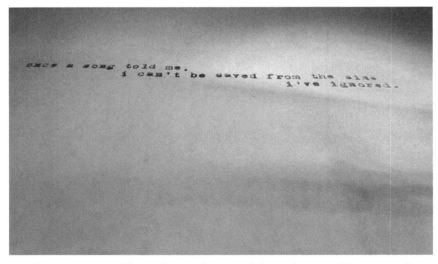

*Once a song told me, I can't be saved from the sins I've ignored.*

*Because I know that I'll fight it for the rest of my life, but I'll make sure I'm having one hell of a time.*

## Love is to Burn

I wish you'd left before I ruined you
Before you'd realized the magnitude of what I was destined to
Wish my mental spitfires weren't hard enough to get through
Wish I was strong enough to pinch the nightmares of personal review

I wasn't me,
Not that I know who I am
You put an end to my conspiracy theories
But you couldn't save me
And perhaps I'm glad
Held your hand through the good and bad
Shielded you from this ocean where I float dormant
If only my hand could have halted the torrent

Pulled every weed in my garden of loneliness
But you came along, insisted I lock the doors of it
Drained my pool of self-deception
Trimmed my thorns and claimed inception

Still, I wasn't clear on foundation
All my friends, shaky ladders of false perception
To be so loved and feel not an inch of it
To patch my holes and still see right through to this

Climbed my ladders of indiscretions
Till I reached the roof
Lit my match of manic overestimation
I know you felt it too
I hope at least, I taught you the lesson
Of how much it hurts to lose
I hope you live a life learning
Never to bend till it all breaks loose

And even more, I hope I taught me

How to see with sighted eyes
And love my blessed miracle
That even I despise
And to read the words scarred in the ash
That seem to mar my clothes:
I know you trimmed our thorns
But we will always have our rose

I wish you'd left before I burned me down

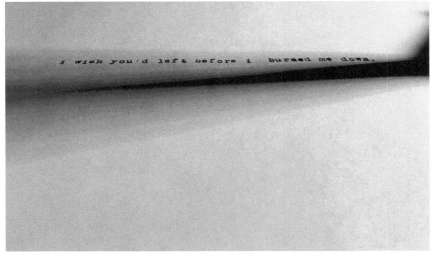

*I wish you'd left before I burned me down.*

# poets dream

One a.m., dog had a seizure last night
Got me thinking about life, like I always do
Perpetual contemplation of existence these days
I guess I need some answers too

Can't tell if what I'm looking for
Is for someone to shine a light in my eyes
Stare at me down from the sewer grates
Show me how it feels to die
Or maybe I do need therapy
Maybe they should just keep me there
Maybe I'd meet some nice people
Some who are just as self-aware

I try to sneak ahead into the future, but I can't
I feel like anything I ponder I ruin with my regret
Future curiosities stained with repercussions from the past
Have every mistake I've ever made on full blast
Replaying these outcomes we don't know exist yet
Show me how to drown without even being wet

Do you remember chasing the raindrops in the dark
And coloring outside the lines?
Do you remember wandering those empty parking lots
Just about noon time?
Do you remember watching the sunset fall over the stables?
We used to eye the water towers from the country roads that you hated
Because it always rained then

I remember me always being the nostalgic one attached to my
bookshelf
Felt too much until I dug a ring of holes around myself
I don't remember asking for help
Doesn't seem like something I'd do

Not when I had so much to lose

Do you remember all those lakeshore vacations?
The first time we ever saw anyone wasted?
I remember watching the people by that trailhead in the sun
And you insisting on filling every silence with horrible puns
Hall & Oates on every speaker
*Maneater*
Watch me wake in a cold sweat
And dwell on the rest of it

Outgrew me, outgrew you
You never quit when it's the right thing to do
Wagon lost its wheels, and we went down with it
My agitation met your obscurity
Overwhelmed with insecurity
We always had that reputation
Of blurring the lines between confidence and uncertainty

I may have left but you walked away
That final glance, then your getaway
Watched the sun rise from the fire tower
Couldn't blame you, went down like a stabbing pill
You try too hard to get it right,
You never truly will

Do you remember naming every constellation?
Listened halfheartedly as my adrenaline slowed
Stared at the sun till it rose
Do you remember all those borrowed clothes?
Wonder why your mind runs so rapidly
But honey, we all know poets dream

And maybe one day you'll meet me in the dark
Tell you I keep cutting my hair short
Find myself wondering how far I could go till I make it

Maybe one day I'll see you in a parking lot about noon
Tell you how your gloom met my doom
Find myself wondering how much longer I can take it

Maybe one day you'll meet me in the old stalls
Eye the water towers from the country roads you hate
A drought this time of year

Find you about the lakeshore
Talk about how in ten years we'll still be here
Maybe we're old enough for that bar
Drink in the sun by that trailhead
Or watch the sky from the towers
I'll wait there for you
Never show but it's okay
Just proving what damage does to you

I'll meet you in the dark, in that empty parking lot
And you'll say it once again
How in our youth we fell for it
Tell me how the horses are doing
And the tower's full of rust
All the dreams we never got
And one day I'll realize
That it's nobody's fault when you both get the same scar
It's okay to run so fast
And never get far

Wonder why my mind runs so rapidly
But honey, we all know poets dream

*Wagon lost its wheels and we went down with it.*

# Questions & Regrets

Venal matter is mind deception
My life sits twisted within these questions
How do you live within this blind inception?
Is living a given if all we're doing is existing?


A blade lodged in my stomach, or at least the feeling
Feel like life is just a nightmare and I'm forever dreaming
Feel like I'm trapped in a dimension between hollowness and meaning
It's so much harder than I thought, living damned of my inevitable caving
I'm wasting


Feel so much pressure to get better; maybe I won't
Boil every time I disappoint you; I have no room to gloat
It's a mystery how I'm even standing, wish I would decompose
But if I do then I'll just leave you to whither alone; maybe that's the goal
Feasting on one last soul, give me a reason to push myself farther from all I've ever known
Because I'm well aware, this pressure is mine to own
Spawn from my brain, a madness I used to call home
Hot, thick, sin puddle beneath my clothes
Wonder when I've ever felt less okay, being alone


Why do I have such a hard time walking away?
Why can I never believe the things that I think and say?
Play it off like I'm just another with some trust issues
But how do you explain that the only thing you don't trust is you?
I try to see the light, but I just thirst for decay
Feed off of my own misery, it's a game that I play


How do I create a life I don't have to routinely escape from?
How the hell do I create a mind that doesn't always feel the need to succumb?

At the end of the day, we're all just searching for things we think will make us heal
But some of us don't last to the end of the day, sometimes the night creeps in and the questions start to reel
How does it feel?

How does it feel knowing that all you ever wanted crumbled beneath your feet?
How does it feel knowing your demons sat you down, rewired your brain in your sleep?
How does it feel knowing your worth dries away every time you admit you can't take the heat?
How does it feel knowing you'll disappoint yourself when your expectations have you beat?

I wish I could tell you how it felt, living a life four years in debt
I wish I tell you after all this time I could stare my demons in the face and not tremble in their threat
I wish I could tell you how many hours of sleep I got back not waking up in a cold sweat
I wish I could tell you that it all gets better; it's just in my head

I wish I could tell you every time I close my eyes I don't dream of my failures
I wish I could tell you every time I stepped outside I didn't recognize the danger
I wish I could tell you that when I get sick I don't ask my demons favors
I wish I could tell you every time I break down I'm not the devil's entertainer
How does it feel?

*I wish I could tell you every time I break down, I'm not the devil's entertainer.*

# Wallflower

Sometimes things are meant to fall apart
Mending isn't the fate of some broken hearts
I wish I could tell you a sad ending went with a happy start
I guess my black and white thinking fell out of love with my black art

It gets heavy sometimes
When you don't read my mind
My inability to communicate has always been ill-timed
My happiness isn't something I really care to find
If not happy then content, living life as it is blind
Your only competition is my stubbornness
And perhaps my wallflower state of mind

I'm out of place
Life isn't really something I want to do any more
These candles melting, more like tears on the floor
Nothing but a mess of atoms with internal eyesores

Been thinking of touch lately
Mind's been wandering out of bounds maybe
Suppose I get curious about situations I don't regard safely
Wonder how fast I'd regret deserting all my safety
It's not something I view quite clearly
Purposely blur the visions, an operation I'm orchestrating
If I don't relax these outside urges
I'm afraid I'll have to restrain me

I admit, quite often I'm lonely
But I'm not big on problem-solving
Self-improvement can get so exhausting
I could argue I'm not one for adapting
Been told my motivation's flattening
I guess this is how it feels to be relapsing
Just another reason to exist unhappily

I suppose it's time to get the bottles of loathe out of safe keeping
After all, what would my hatred do without me?

There's no better time than the present
Why be so near when you could be distant?
I'll hand you the shovel, bury me beneath the cement
I hope it dries before I relive the discontent
Just deplete the air, I don't want to be reminded of the segments
All the time drained by this irreparable torment

It's funny how the voices have so much self-esteem
They sure know how to live life, never having done anything
I'm living life avoiding all the remedies
Shortening the time I have to spend with me
Who needs peace when you can live off trickery?

I'm high off my head
I'm sorry if it's startling
Just don't forget
The temptresses, how they start circling
You'll get a glimpse
Of all the happiness they've been harvesting
Unsettling, isn't it,
How quickly you'll start spiraling?

I've come to contemplate if emotions are meant for healing
I'd rather get some detached attention without the grief of feelings
This boulevard of retrospect, I walk forever bleeding
The wallflower has come home
And she's not keen on forgiving

*Mending isn't the fate of some broken hearts.*

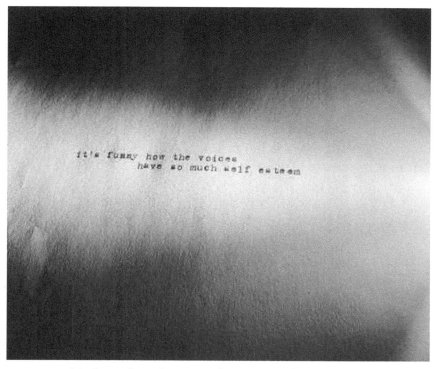

*It's funny how the voices have so much self-esteem.*

# *orchid*

I'm a really hard person to love, aren't I?
I don't think about it much
But it comes out when I use my sensitivity as a crutch—
A firing squad of all my sins and mistakes,
A replica of the fears I can't erase
It's quite an embarrassing thing to confess:
How come my self-love dries when I split open
But I don't love you any less?

I know it's hard to tell, I'm determined to work through it
I try to speed the progress, but I'm caged in this slow-motion
I know you think I'm wasted, I'm good at the impression
It's hard to talk about it, you'll give me an expectation
I'm tired of going to bed with all these knots of tension
I'm tired of insulting love with all these chaotic notions

I didn't say goodbye
I know I should regret it
I left so long before I said the words
Last thing on my mind was etiquette
All the hours I spent waiting,
The nights I'd lie up breaking
I said goodbye in all the words I wasn't saying

It's the impulsive need that really gets me angry
How I feel I have to disagree with everything
Just to grasp a chunk of lost identity
My default personality is worn from all the empathy

I don't want to be your lost cause;
I hope you keep counting those stars

I hope I didn't dead-end your road
It's a lie to say that I'm better off alone
I was so scared of your judgement,
I couldn't stay afloat—
The asphalt of my mind again,
How this dome comes crumbling down again
I'm not human; I'm a heartache with no home

So I hope you wipe your feet off on someone else's door
 'Cause I'm not here for you any more

How could you love something no one would dream of being?
I smile sometimes but happiness isn't worth my reaching
I guess I just got let down
Took your fake love and spit it out
Been waiting for rain in this endless drought
Our flowers, they've been wilting
Our memories, they've been shrinking
We both know hearts, how they heal from breaking

Don't think of it as time wasted
All of the pain, my fault for chasing it
Heart's heading home to dry out
No remedies could save it now
I ran too far to be an artist
I forgot where we started
Now our hearts, aren't they guarded?
Our temperatures turned arctic

I'll rest our stone in the garden
Can we thaw it, all that's hardened?
At least we didn't live deserted
Our history will always be recorded
I'm sorry I killed us before we could bloom like an orchid

I wouldn't survive you a second time,
So please stay away from here
Draw an X on the map like the bullet in my back,
And please stay away from here

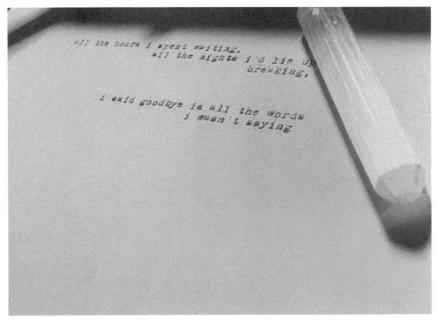

*All the hours I spent waiting, all the nights I'd lie up breaking; I said goodbye in all the words I wasn't saying.*

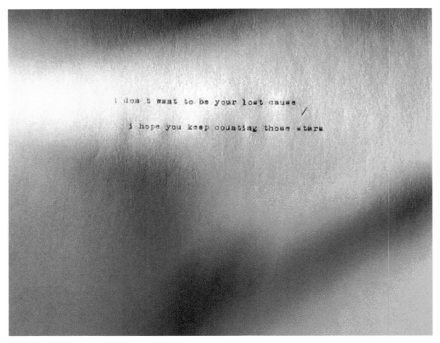

*I don't want to be your lost cause; I hope you keep counting those stars.*

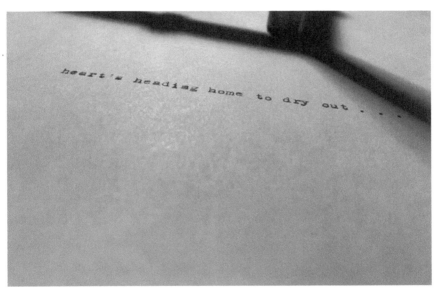

*Heart's heading home to dry out...*

# *half girl*

Watch me pace in circles, drawing the lines
Panic, a boulder in the pebble of time
Add bricks to every wall I've had to climb
Things we all have to deal with a million times
Waiting until I reach the point of maximum danger—
I hear it's pretty weightless up there

Strong, the side of me I rarely know
Too busy overanalyzing old circumstances, old habit that won't go
Funny how I can hardly remember when I hit the point of no control
But I could draw a map of how it felt, an X in every torn hole

 Half Heaven, Half Hell: See the devil clench the bars of its cell
I see it now, how every broken stitch drew you well
Searching for answers but lost in your questions
Watched you surrender on the night that you failed
Tried to bargain with light
But now we see which side prevailed

I know I did all the things to you I said I never would
And now I blame you for believing the words "I could"
Prisoner of dread, how could you have been fooled?
Didn't know you had so much blood until it pooled
You watch me circle the lines I drew in my youth; seems you're being
ridiculed
Anger's too slow to flare, looks like you're overruled

Watch the council take the vote
Your last plea, a solemn note
Couldn't hear over the cheers
But your end was far from near

Dead eyes, gray, graze along the horror
Reach into the darkness and take what you can bargain for

I'd like to think your fate is something you have to earn;
Truth is, you never really learned

Allow me to escort you to your newfound homeland
Where everything you ogle is a brain-distorted dead-end
Hope you cave in before anyone tells the legend
Of the girl who danced with her indiscretions
And befriended the depression
Of the sea of Half Heaven, Half Hell—
Where this water quenches the thirst of innocents
Inundates those of fickleness,
Where the Half Girl rests in her cloak of sea swell

If only she could have outswum her dry spell

*Didn't know you had so much blood until it pooled.*

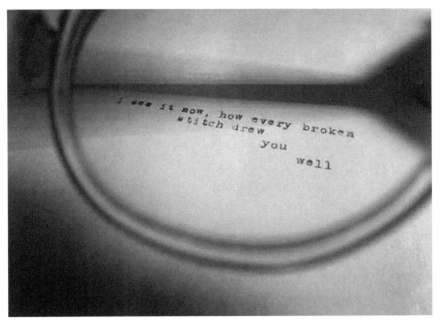

*I see it now, how every broken stitch drew you well.*

# There Will Be Peace

Growing increasingly exhausted with repackaging the same message
Growing increasingly exhausted with never seeming to come down
from the ledge
There's no formal way to express the concept, with all the things it
suggests
Truly I think the most terrifying part is you becoming the byproduct of
it

What's been revealed so far is its unwillingness to swim against the
current
There truly is no way to fight it other than to drown it from your
conscience
It's not that my demons swim; it's that they are the whole ocean
And they snatch me from the surface and choke me with every motion
It's not that I don't try or that I'm completely helpless
It's just the pain of being sucked dry and returning with nothing left

Overthinking so much that now it has me ill
Try to drown it a couple times with some out-of-date prescription pills
The way I'd describe it is like a headache you just can't shake
Except you lie awake helpless amidst the agony, hoping you're a
mistake

It's only a chemical imbalance
I know I'm on the road to recovery
I just can't help feeling like all my terrors are doing is enlivening
I know it's not simple, but I didn't anticipate this kind of pain
I know it's the road to recovery but it's kind of feeling like the highway
to hell

I've felt everything and nothing and I can't decide which is worse
One is sopping wet and hopelessness and everything really hurts
The other's brutally dry, leaves you in an indescribable thirst
With no tears left to produce and it all feels like an illusion

Leaves me bargaining with death, at least then I would get some rest in

I hate writing about it only to have no solution
Like a position paper with a flimsy, unsettling conclusion
You can expand on an unsolved issue to your heart's content
But I fear I do not yearn for awareness or acceptance
Just an ounce of peace and you'll never hear from me again
Except for when I'm back to bother you by the time winter rolls in

I know my soul chooses to feel these things
I guess mine's just sadistic
Nobody wants to accept that sometimes things are meant to go bad
Sometimes we take bad things because they're the only things we ever had
I guess I just want you to know that sadness isn't a flaw
More like a never-ending, anxiety-riddled street brawl
In the darkest alley imaginable and everyone has a gun
New in town, look around, you thought everything was gonna be fun

I know how freeing it feels to be happy
I just wish I felt it more often
It's honestly pretty pitiful to sit and watch how everything caves in
Hate myself for feeling relief whenever I feel happy
Just reminds me of what I'm hardly capable of and it only gets me thinking
About how we all wish for normal but it's truly an illusion
I guess I should use the word "functional"; it seems more exact
I mean, you could have a balanced brain and still be racist in 2020
But please don't be fooled, your brain is gone and now all we can do is pity

I guess I should just start congratulating myself on simple decency
I guess I gotta remember all I am so I can get back to me
Suppose I'm just fearful I'll remind myself
And be unhappy at the realization that I'm all I have
My greatest dream is to calm down and be proud of who I am

But sometimes, understand, nothing ever goes to plan

Sometimes I wish I could sit me down
Look me in the eye, say, "Child, you make me proud
But sometimes you gotta know to settle down
Step back, look around, take it all in now
I know you think you deserve this pain but somehow you don't
At the end of your rope, I know you think that's self-centered though

"I can promise you, you are naturally kind
Clouded capacity and invalidation just get in the way sometimes
Say it with me now, suffering is not a contest
I know you think your pain's invalid 'cause you drowned sooner than the rest
But your pain is real and accepted and it means something
Child, trust me, a light is coming to overshadow your darkening

"Stop right now, being ashamed of feeling so much
You are not oversensitive; you are open and that is enough
You apologize and forgive yourself for feeling lesser than
And blindly welcoming your enemies like a doorman
And yes, you're fully responsible for the expectation you created for yourself
You will hold yourself accountable for the pain you have caused others
Intentional or not, you scarred their sun with rain and thunder

"I know you feel your health is fading and it's only a matter of time
But you are learning to be happy and whole again, don't let it go by
You will escape the default personality you created for yourself
That was just your mind's way of telling you it really needed your help

"Don't you worry about being too much, Mom and Dad knew what they were doing
Took you home from the hospital that day, they knew you could never be perfect
Had no expectation of precision, that was always you doing too much

No need to suppress your problems to lessen their load
Learning how to stop purchasing this guilt from expired barcodes

"You will write your own conclusion
You will escape from yourself
You will release fears of making friends
Worried they'll wander your baggage and leave you on the shelf
Child, if they can't handle your issues, they don't deserve your wellness
It's really a simple cause: cherish yourself and trust the process

"You are beautiful and resilient
You release the urgency
To match the energy of those who don't care to solve their problems
I know you examine people and always think it's your job to solve
them

"Right now, release every thought telling you it's your job to do
everything for everyone
It's not your job to walk their path, they have to learn to do what's best
And stop believing that you're mean
Whenever you say 'no' to literally anything
It's your mind's instinctive reaction to put you in their shoes
And create false realities of what others think of you

"You are lively and energetic in every single step
You are wise beyond your years and have an indescribable depth
You walk through all life's issues and come out the other side
And I'm sorry you spent so many years living just to die

"But you're doing great
There are just a couple things that you must know—
I'll make it quick, I know you care enough to listen, though—
You just have to trust me when I say there's enough air to breathe
And there is enough hope for everyone in this world, including me
And I will make it back one day, it's my mission to succeed
And child, I promise you when I'm done, there will be peace"

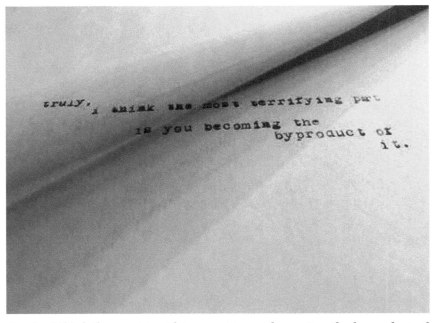

*Truly, I think the most terrifying part is you becoming the byproduct of it.*

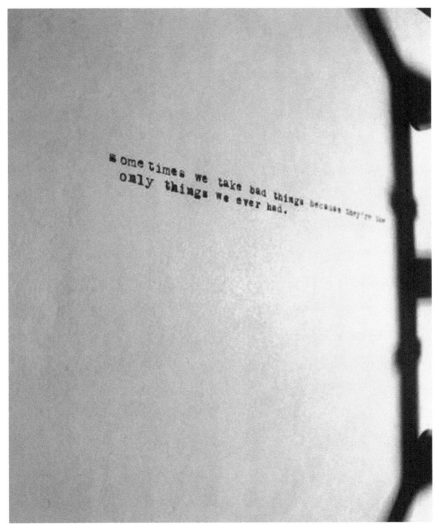

*Sometimes we take bad things because they're the only things we ever had.*

## me & my ghost

Why can't you just let me live for a while?
I think it's time your thoughts lower the dial
Why do you have to close every open door?
Why do you shut your eyes when you're near
All you've been looking for?

Backspace the message if you think of texting me
Erase my contact, we aren't all we're meant to be
Delete the screenshots you saved in insincerity
Remember how I "kept you from your dreams"?
I'm sure you're pondering on that now
All the books of memories,
They'll tunnel their way back into your head somehow

Stay gone, it's not hard for me to say it
How hard is it for energy to be reciprocated?
Our contract has been permanently terminated
I'll write the pages of our end
My mom was right, you really are just my "little friend"

Watch me as I quickly fade
The earth flies, our sweet grenade
I guess our inevitable was just delayed
You wore a mask of who you portrayed
You never truly saw my face,
Did you?

It's time I sail to a different coast
If our distance is what you treasure the most
I invite you to stop scrutinizing my life from your observation post
Would you prefer I clean my bedroom for you,
Since you ought to be my little ghost?

Stand down, it's not wise to start debating

My language, it got lost in your translating
Don't wait for the news to start circulating
The press believes they're invading
How would I explain that it's just me & my ghost?

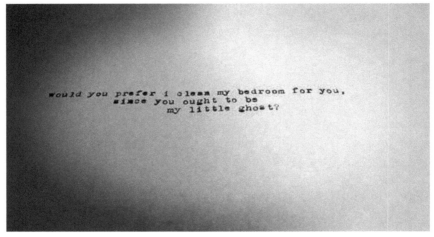

*Would you prefer I clean my bedroom for you, since you ought to be my little ghost?*

# *childhood revival*

Oh child,
I fear I know your struggle
Of growing up too soon
Just want to stare up at the ceiling
See all the popcorn making friends
And watch the ceiling fan swirl in my regret
The summer of childhood retrospect

Cold year, I've learned not to fear the warnings
They're bitterer than most
Long night, long year of signals
Can't go a day without a disconnect
Say yes, say no, I don't know
Don't want to talk to anyone
Wonder why I tear myself down
To be built back up again
Dissociation has the face of a loaded gun
And I'm not scared to die

Change, the only constant
I must remain constant with it
I have no choice but to sink, to swim
Just stay afloat
Sing every note, even if it's off-key
I wasn't built to be good at everything
Let's take a drive to New York City
Make a week out of it
Get back, sit down, and realize
I finally have no regrets

Cruel year, they've learned not to fear the warnings
They're harder than they seem
Let go, stand tall, no weakness
I guess they have a façade for everything

For years, they're driving across the country
Searching for some peace
Blind eyes and riptides and failure
All these lives never looked so empty

And when they're mad for no reason
And everything at once
Makes them feel like they'll never get back again

I will be home in the morning
And we'll rewrite the page
Scribble out everything unimportant
That you ponder on these days
Tough year, I know it hurts you
It's just the typical way
Of bending till it breaks you
Have to shatter, it's the only way to get through

Oh child,
I fear I know your heartache
Of trusting life too soon
Find that every trip-up
It always gets to you
Stand back, see it well
All the colors of the sunset
Want to paint a pretty picture, with all of your regret?

I used to think I didn't know my bridges
Until I burned them all down
But with sighted eyes I can say
I've never been more proud
My bridges withstand all my love, now an innocent weight
And I smile 'cause nothing's felt the same
Since I realized my fate

Ask me what I value

Answer doesn't come right away
Why is it so hard to think of the words I want to say?
Have a general image
Have to write it all down
And with my head above water
I think I can make it back somehow

And when I'm mad for no reason
And everything at once
Makes me feel like I'll never get back again,
I prove myself right
That all along the problem was me
All these realizations—
Things no one can steal from me
My head is above water now

I stare up at the ceiling
See all the popcorn making friends
And watch the ceiling fan swirl in my progress
The summer of childhood revival

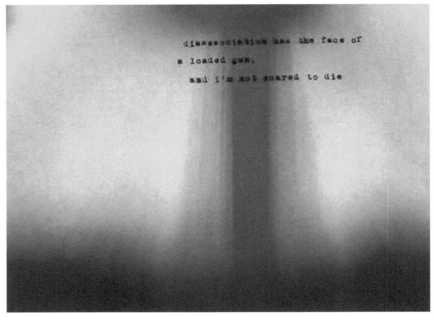

*Disassociation has the face of a loaded gun, and I'm not scared to die.*

*All these lives never looked so empty.*

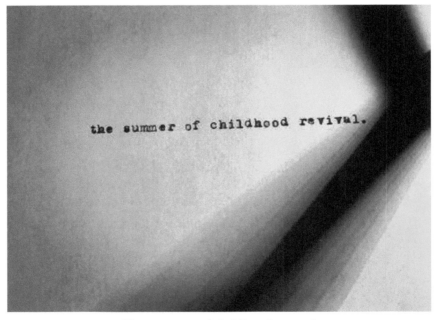

*The summer of childhood revival.*

# Die in dignity

I don't want to write, I want to die
I guess I expected you to fix a problem that was never yours
I guess I'll keep wandering these playing fields
Trying to settle my scores

Sometimes things just happen
Sometimes things just fall apart
I think my faucet's broken
Spitting out emotions I didn't even know exist
I'm still trying to figure it out;
The abyss,
Is it as tempting as I think?

There's nothing that I have left to hide
It's morning
I guess I have no time to die
I'm tired
Of getting midnight thoughts in daytime
I hope no one ever feels like this
I'll be the last with a story like mine

Maybe it's a fake addiction
Maybe I should rewrite the laws—
"required reciprocation"
You think that'll get me attention?

Not harboring feelings feels morally irresponsible
These emotions aren't even plausible
How come they always feel so tangible?
Looks like I've made myself another obstacle
It's exhausting, feelings have become so untranslatable
I thought you knew my language
But I guess it's impermissible

Sometimes things just happen
Sometimes things just fall apart
I've become a broken record
I don't want you in fits and starts
Now I'm forcing pieces that I know don't fit
Perhaps I could stick them with my bleeding heart

I know I'm worth something
I just don't know what it is yet
I hope searching doesn't put me in debt
Passed around, there's a story that's been told:
Pain can turn you kind or it can turn you mean
I guess I got a little bit of both

How do I forgive myself for everything I didn't become?
Everything that can never be undone
I guess it's a battle that's never won
And one day we'll all be picked off one by one
By our own perceptions
Tell me, will you be willing?

Sometimes things just happen
Sometimes things just fall apart
And I'm one of them
We're all one of them

Just show up as you
I guess we're gonna keep pretending until it all makes sense
But it's a dangerous thing,
To put stock in something that's not guaranteed
Just because you think that's how it's supposed to be

I already told you:
I don't care if I die in pain
As long as I die in dignity

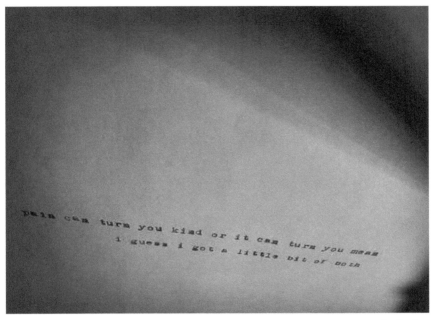

*Pain can turn you kind or it can turn you mean; I guess I got a little bit of both.*

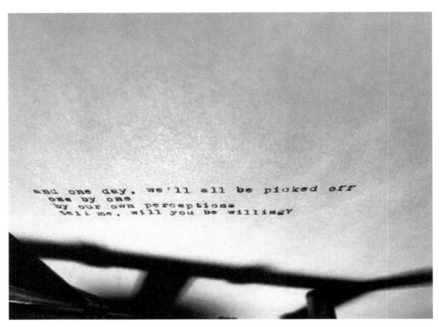

*And one day, we'll all be picked off one by one by our own perceptions.*
*Tell me, will you be willing?*

# *landing*

We can't know what everything means
Sometimes there isn't a message behind the simple things
I wish I knew how to say it subtly
How it all pours out so unsteadily

Trusting me is like believing a feather in the wind won't tremble
Loving me is like getting flashbacks of things you don't want to
remember
But hurting me is like warming in these burning embers
Who knew one wounded mind held such a rampant storm center?

Influenced by people who mean well,
Telling me how everything I need is already inside myself
Only makes me harbor this anger even tighter to my chest
How do I punish the world for making me believe I'm nothing if I'm
not the best?

Trying to learn to stop forcing things
I've been told I come off a bit controlling
Should I make the excuse that it's because upstairs is in need of repair?
It's not really living when you know you're not going anywhere

We're all alone in our own ways, I know that
Feel self-centered whenever I'm too fogged in my thoughts, I can't
control that
Don't have enough energy to put it all back in the past
I don't resist the notion that my mind is something proven unsurpassed

I know I'm not enough; you've taught me that
All your little lessons, did they sink in at last?
Now you have me sitting here making excuses in this intervention
Now you have me spending my teenage years undoing the
transfiguration

No, I don't hate you
It's worse than that
You stole my life and I want it back
I shove it down until it balloons in my throat
You may have stolen my time, but I'm the one that let you go
How you walked away so unscathed
Now you live your life never paying for how you behaved
Meanwhile I have to unpack all my baggage to people I don't know
I have to sit here and let everyone know how paranoid you can grow
Now I have to repair an existence I don't even care to mend
It's called being resented, don't ask me again

How early you learned to hate people
Makes me wonder how you're doing now, making a sequel?
I have this anger in my heart that I can't contain
Put me through all this hell, and what did you gain?
What, did it make you powerful and empty you of your emotional drain?
What, did you think we would be even if I felt your pain?

Truth is, I do feel sorry for your actions
You took your jealousy and belittled how good you had it
I'm still not even sure what it was that you wanted
How did puncturing my life make you any less haunted?
Makes me wonder what went up in your house that was so daunting
What rage did they make you bottle that you projected at those that stood by watching?

Turns out all your paradise did was make you deprived
Did they make you harden up only to drench you in lies?
How did you get so overcome in the evil where you reside?
Well now I have to spend the rest of my life mourning the death of someone who's still alive

All your toxicity did was spark a playground rebellion

Don't come around and tell me this pain will make me the bigger
person
Don't even try to sell the reality that you had such good intentions
You live a life running for your life but it's nothing you want to
mention
I'm not convinced you did it all just for some flimsy attention
Something went up in that house I was always jealous of
But now I see you were the one living a young life unloved
And I sincerely hope, for your sake, it's something that can become
undone

"It's not your job to save anyone but yourself"
You spun that quote, pitched your hate till we were parallel
Now all that's left to do is live as long as I'll let me
Pick up the pieces and make myself feel worthy
Sound, my mind will be eventually:
All worlds return by morning
And you'll spy my shadow looming
Don't look now, you've been fearing my coming
This wondrous mess is set for landing

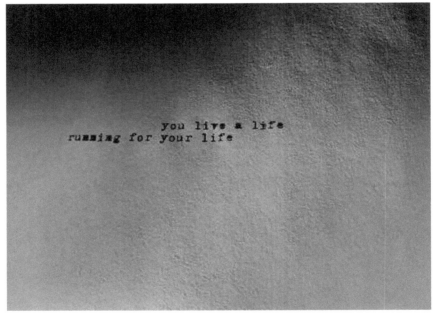

*You live a life running for your life.*

*All worlds return by morning. (I'll see you soon.)*

*sad // healed*

Running on an empty gas tank
My mind's a blank void
This heart is getting heavy
Feel like an android
I have come here to conquer
All that makes me paranoid
I see your lips are moving
Can't hear over this noise

Living on that low percentage
I guess I'm taking my time
Skimming through the acid dreams
Of my unconscious mind
I've had a lifetime of being alone
They say I'm hard to find
I've lived a life with one heartbeat
But now it's falling behind

Smear this world of stainless steel
Running from my ego ideals
Stop by my grave at the potter's field

I see me shaking in those thick crowds
And those voices, something I can never drown out
I guess maybe emptiness is my friend now

My mind has become a breeding ground
All these stitches have left me unsound
Spend myself chasing those doubt clouds
Maybe the sky would clear in some other town

Smear this world of stainless steel
Running from my ego ideals
Stop by my grave at the potter's field

When trepidation sends me letters now,
I leave the seals intact like I'm not around
On the train tracks heading for eastbound
This war, we'll find a middle ground

And we'll smear this world of stainless steel
Running from my ego ideals
Stop by my grave at the potter's field
I may be sad
But I am healed

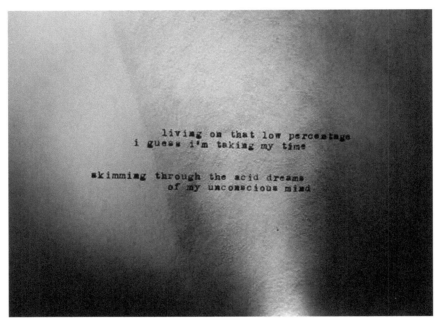

*Living on that low percentage, I guess I'm taking my time skimming through the acid dreams of my unconscious mind.*

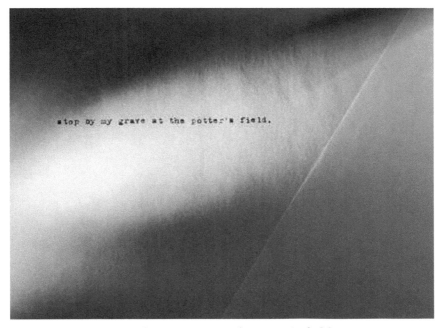

*Stop by my grave at the potter's field.*

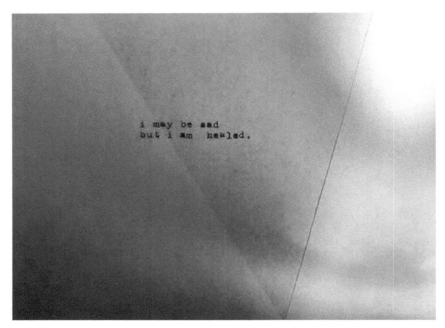

*I may be sad but I am healed.*

# *reminders*

Asking questions to ceilings
Maybe you'll get your answer tonight
You've been apologizing a lot lately
Don't think the timing's ever right
How long had you been holding out
Finally, before you broke down?
We're going to get there just fine
Time may not heal, but it can be redefined

I see the light at the end of the tunnel
And I'm going to make you see
I know that void you've been stuffing
But I'm going to make you believe
I know you've been fighting fire with fire
I think it's about time you won
And I know you hate this world
You're not the only one

I know you hate the way
You got your finger on that self-destruct
Doesn't reality have the face
Of a loaded gun?
I know you can't see eye-to-eye
With what you've become
And if you're going to cry
At least cry on company time

Could you leave it all overseas?
Could you run before you sink too deep?
Knowing then what you know now,
Would you still have leaped?
Heart's a little swollen but we'll give it time
How flammable egos become under knowing minds

How strong you must be to exist in this grief
But you can admit it's overwhelming
When all you do is think
I see that scar in your back when you fell over your heels
I see that hole in your heart when you strived for appeal
I know that look in your eyes, concealing the emotions you feel
When did you start building your life on an unachievable ideal?

When you're walking those wires with a blindfold;
When you're pulling those teeth, living life unsold;
When you admit circumstance is too much to withhold;
When you're watching the fabric of time unfold;
You don't need me to tell you—
You already know—
But I'll keep whispering the reminders
That you are solid gold

*Asking questions to ceilings; maybe you'll get your answer tonight.*

# The visionary

I'm not afraid of peace;
I'm afraid of change
But peace and change, you see,
Live adjoined in my world of division,
Twin moons in this sky of day,
Breathing spirited among the inspirited
Beyond me their intention when they torch these woods I roam
Piggy-eyed portals of ink, my introspection they call home

Should they splinter this dome with web-like shards of what time
couldn't spare,
I'll be wrestling with my eyes,
Ogling existence as a wounded solider muttering his last prayer

The words, they reek of repudiation, his determination gone stale,
For circumstance had stripped him far too young,
Deprived of opportunity to prevail;
His strength does not lie in a stretch of land in which his loyalties be
tested;
His mind shall shame this battlefield,
Where the visionary is nested

Indefinitely blank, his eyes center on the sky:
A scattered labyrinth of white; sometimes clouds aren't meant to look
like anything
But it is these notions that denied him a candidate as the inner child
who survived;
We scorch our bliss with these epiphanies in hopes that fate would
materialize

He notices, these days are prolonging longer now
Caged around the truth as these lies are fading out
Do humans take it for granted, not living in a bubble?
Truly a wonder how the sun persists above his stark eyes

The moment he hopes for night to linger
To mask the struggle raging inside

This infinite sea of desperation does blaze in his mind,
How foolishly he ran away from things that never left:
*Feed me to the wolves before I bear to do it myself.*

After all, it's hard closing a door that never truly opened:
Those twin moons of bloodlust come to signal when the hope ends
He wonders when he started watching it ring instead of picking up the
phone
Oh, how he thought he held the past—
But it was him within its hold
He had banished himself to remembrance, telling the stories he's
already told
But he knew deep down desperation's tide is a pool that would never
smooth
How accustomed he'd become to always bending the ugly, evil truth

How adjoined peace and change be;
How disjointed death is looming
However, living was never his cup of tea
So what path shall be lain before he?
Exhausted of wandering aimlessly,
So he shall come to you, change,
In his sinful search of holy peace
These ash trees shall retract their whispers of uncertainty
He'll rally these frayed troops with their vigorous apathy

And he understands it now,
Such a sacred prophecy:
You could drain the body but never the visionary

*Oh, how he thought he held the past but it was him within its hold.*

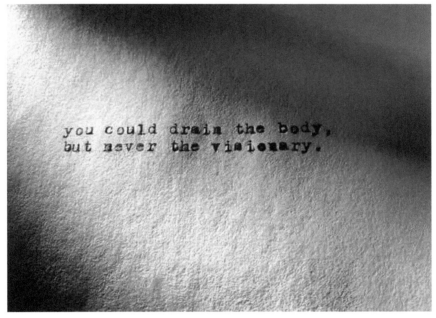

*You could drain the body, but never the visionary.*

# *looking glass*

There is no better way to die
Than to die telling the truth
Sit and ponder who scorched the world you believed was eternal
Peer through the looking glass and it all comes back to you

It's been a few years of my life
Perhaps I'm dying by design
And maybe I'll get broken down
Find my corpse along a pier,
But I will live with the knowledge
At least I did not crumble here

I never told you, did I?
How I had so much to lose
Don't think I ever mentioned
How estranged I've become to you
And you had never noticed
The letters I had written into the ground
Have you grown hard of hearing,
Or had my emptiness not made a sound?

I don't feel loved, not any more
These waves have been creeping inshore
Quick, don't look now—
Don't see me shake; I don't want to let you down

Hope I don't make it worse
Need me gone, just let me know
I'm already miles away

You won't be surprised
Anyway, I've been wasting all your time
Traipse down the hall
Two open eyes, a single glance

And then you're gone

I'll wash in the creek
And I will count the stars in which I had placed my dreams
I'll bring along some needles and thread
And hem my clothes when it gets warm again

I only made it worse
I'll live with what I deserve
I'm already miles away

I won't be surprised
By how quickly hurt can magnetize
And I'll be unashamed
And fearless, like I was then that night

I guess I'm not above grudges:
As long as I'm alive
My mistakes are recognized
My lies will materialize
And I hope you replay yours all the time
Truly a mystery
How you could even think
That blood would excuse all that's damaging
You've already given me the memories
Of how I can't disagree
But I still disagree
This fountain I swim is now a wellspring

Was I all you ever wanted me to be?
You built me out of fear, and I will come
I will come be what I needed when I was young
When I was young and unashamed and fearless
Like I was then that night

And so I wash my soul of riptides in the creek
And I wait for the sharp shadows of night to speak
But I am old and unashamed and fearless
Like I was then that night

There is no better way to die
Than to die telling the truth
Sit and ponder who scorched the world you believed was eternal
You peered through the looking glass
And it all came back to you

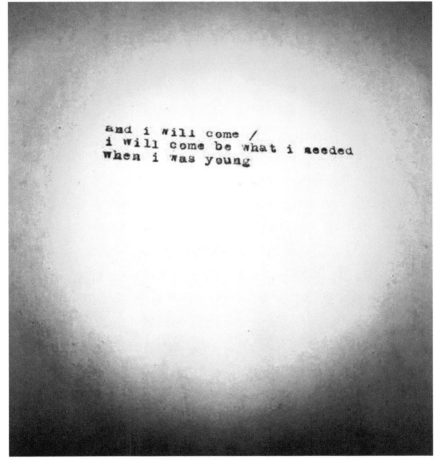

*And I will come, I will come be what I needed when I was young.*

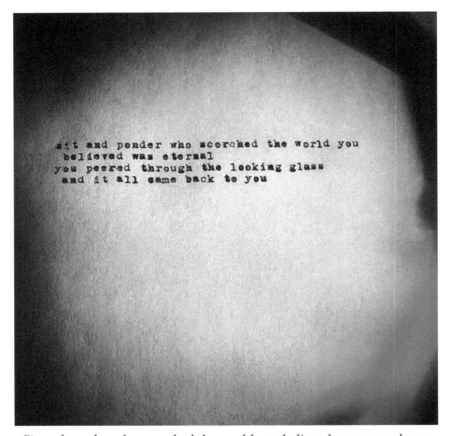

*Sit and ponder who scorched the world you believed was eternal; you peered through the looking glass and it all came back to you.*

## *it doesn't have to make sense*

Remember when we used to live like it was nothing
Now we just fall apart like it's nothing
Skipping rocks down by the river's edge
When we'd not break, but bend
And the sun would come back up again
And those engines start rumbling

It was quite the view from up here
Out in the mornings I see the sierra clear
And in the fields I eye your burned-out circuit
Why do we always look at what we deserve
And try to desert it?

So you're going to sit around until it all makes sense?
You're going to wait until you plow into your dead-end?
You turned a blind eye to your dividend
Gifted with the stubbornness of a fisherman's bend

And I know that you're never going to put it to rest
All the outcomes that you replay inside of your head
And there's so much to be said
But you don't trust the words of your mind
I wish you would just shatter the clock
And wait for time

There is never a right time to be left;
The only thing we left was time
Of course, there's nothing easier to deny
Than living life breathing for a lie

You begged her to hang around
But the floorboards through which her soul had seeped
Whispered a fortune derived from the heart of a machine:
You'll see her when you fall asleep

A love in which the cut was you
And the blood was her
Forever oozing
But with no succor
And you had never felt more alive
But such a love is suicide

So you're going to sit around until it all makes sense?
You're going to wait until you plow into your dead-end?
Well let me let you in on a little secret:
Nothing is ever going to make sense
And it doesn't have to

And there will come a time
When you'll see through the ruse
I know you don't trust the waters
But these steady ships will carry your heart
Back to you

*I wish you would just shatter the clock and wait for time.*

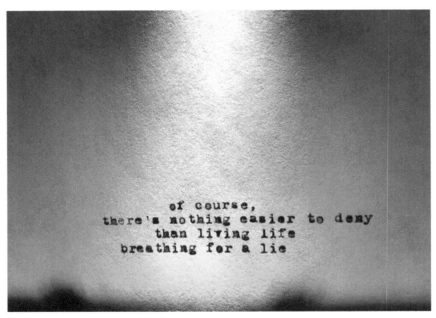

*Of course, there's nothing easier to deny than living life breathing for a lie.*

i know you don t trust these waters

but these steady ships will carry
your heart
back to you

*I know you don't trust these waters but these steady ships will carry
your heart back to you.*

## my crown is made of warning signs

If it's what I deserve than why should I escape it?
Spend my days getting bit on my bad tendon
And scratching my skin until it splits
Blood comes rushing out again until my head's trapped in your orbit
But not my heart

And it still hurts
That I bleed you
That I'll never let you go
That this spinning has me dizzy and faint
But I'd still take the midnight train
Back home

Your pace is quickening
Your vision's sharpening
Your luggage rolling
It's ten till twelve

You left your beanie
Right where you left me
The rain is beating
Try to squint through the prints
I guess we'll have to learn how to coexist

How come now you're unraveling?
Perhaps you had it coming
And it came—loud and clear
Mumbled apologies and heavy breathing
And a slight ringing in your ear

And it still hurts
That you bleed me
That you'll never let me go
But at least you've got me spinning

And I'll breathe slower
As I enter the world below

Do you want to spend the night?
How about we spend our lives?
You can never be ready to be left
And maybe that's not the half of it
But my head's heavy now,
Your voice a distant sound
My mind's the darkest cloud
And you see it now,
As you're zoning out
Leaning on the windowpane
And you'll stop by the bar car and grab yourself a drink
And maybe I'll try to bide my time
But we all know a new mind's a new game

And you'll get bored and flip through my discography
And think I'm up to my ears in manic energy
But it's never what you think;
It's the thing that strings us all together,
The last thing the voices want to fester
While I am not a fortune teller,
One day you'll see

The conductor's voice is ringing
The crowd has begun thinning
And I am so near weeping
I step in the bar car and order a drink

Spend my days getting bit on my bad tendon
And scratching my skin until it splits
Blood comes rushing out again until my head's trapped in your orbit
But not my heart

And your eyes flicker open
And there's so much pain
And so much love
And we let us zip it up
I guess my air supply didn't keep you alive long enough

And my head's heavy now
Your voice a distant sound
And finally, the truth seeps out

My crown is made of warning signs

blood comes rushing out again until my head's
trapped in your orbit.
but not my heart.

*Blood comes rushing out again until my head's trapped in your orbit.*
*But not my heart.*

*Do you want to spend the night? How about we spend our lives?*

*A new mind's a new game.*

# Avenue

I hummed our song on the old country roads
Coming back from walking you home
I skipped loose pebbles behind your house's face
You have no idea the little dance I did in your driveway

You tell me it won't hurt
But I still remember the look on your face
And the dimly lit shop backing highway 98
There's still some nail on your lips
From where you bit it off
And you didn't cry; instead, you mocked the time
They said you'd never be enough

And my ears were ringing over all of the noise
Cursing over all of the wires and machines you couldn't avoid
My muddied shoelaces scraped the tiled floors
From when I'd tripped over myself trying to get my hand into yours

You tell me it won't hurt
But I still remember the way
That you didn't cry the times we circled the drain
You didn't need morphine; you'd kill your pain

It was a Tuesday we'd hauled all the boxes
Out from under my bed, like months ago I had promised
And I strung you together in all the old pictures
And I picked my favorite out of the litter
The old carpet's an accent to the light in your eyes
I never took many pictures of you
I'm still wondering why

Just after dark the car skids to a stop
Flung the door open and bolted down the block
You were murmuring some lyrics I didn't know you knew

You were wrapped in a shield I couldn't see through
And now I know you clear as day:
You were just trying to memorize the smell of the rain
And I remember thinking,

What is life without you;
What is you without pain?

I'm sorry about a lot of things
But this one the most
We thought we'd beat the winter
But our flower valley froze
And I wonder, the look on your face
If you could see me now,
Swallowing the love I didn't know was around

I still have trouble trusting beginnings
It always feels like something is missing;
Maybe there's a hole in my chest that has just opened up
I may have unclogged the drain but I'm still sore from us
And I look back and remember the memories I'd missed
I suppose beginnings are only half-lived

*There's still some nail on your lips from where you bit it off, and you didn't cry; instead, you mocked the time they said you'd never be enough.*

*You didn't need morphine; you'd kill your pain.*

## I love you

The ice water melts fast
I've come to reason that you just aren't coming back
I thought you would've, but I can't see through you yet
Thought I couldn't get lower than this
Turns out Hell has a basement

You say my mind haunts me
So I'll just haunt it back
Your intentions I could never track
I wish I could hate you like that;
I blame you for the fragility of my heart
These days it never stays intact

You were like a cup of coffee:
Not so much about drinking you but having you around
Never talked but our minds made the sounds
I wonder what you would've sounded like
Coming out of your mouth

It's not hard to want to,
But it's hard to keep you
Shattered my heart and picked out a shard
Just to break down your walls
But you just kept climbing that tower
And I was never one to stay

These midnight thoughts keep crowding my day
I'm skipping this chapter of this story of mine
And you'll write yours without me
And maybe you'll think sometimes
How loving someone back would be

This mind is dead like I am to you;
It's not a threat but a promise that I'll get through

And in my times of desperation,
I'll be sure to picture that old hotel room
How you finished everything we started
And I was born anew

But I don't live life for reciprocation
I do not breathe to be drawn into submission
And if I sat with a dictionary at our old booth
And looked up the word "damnation",
It would read you

I piece together the shards of my heart
I broke for you
And I clear this mind that all at once
Bled blue
No worries, dear,
I'll have the automated voice say, "I love you"

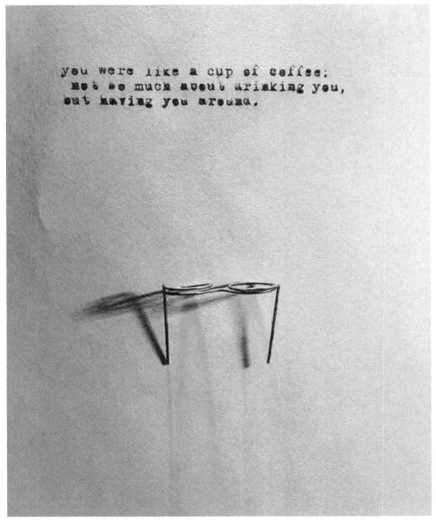

*You were like a cup of coffee: not so much about drinking you, but having you around.*

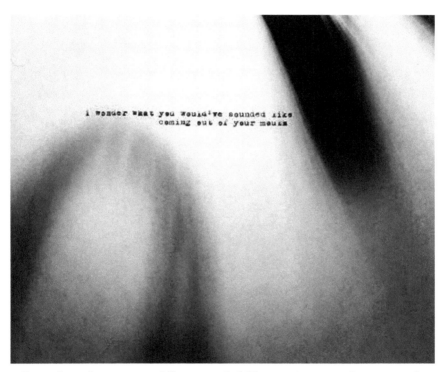

*I wonder what you would've sounded like coming out of your mouth.*

*It's not hard to want to, but it's hard to keep you.*

*we are infinite*

Have you ever seen yourself up close?
Not in a mirror, but in the sky
As the moon drifts over these canyon waters
Something cosmic broke the day you left
The moon winked out of the sky;
You always did sleep in pitch black

Have you ever seen yourself from someone else's point of view?
We are misconception bodies, but one mind of breakthroughs
It's a strange thing, to finally admit you walk this earth
With billions of bodies and stars and clouds
But one mind, alone

Have you ever been compared to dirt?
Marketed and advertised and sold and judged
And the check gets split between the sum of us
We don't yet know what to do to earn our trust
To admit that there is no difference
And hate always comes barging in
And we spend our nights counting our sins
Our rose died before it could bloom, didn't it?

Have you ever seen the universe repair a gap in her weaving?
Imagine if seven billion hearts stopped beating
Imagine if all the birds in the sky went fleeing
But you were just in the shower, singing
As the universe fell
That's a gap more universal than the universe
But we are the rulers of the cosmos
And you're dead weight on the bathroom floor
Watch your cloud kingdom vanish forevermore

Have you ever dressed up for yourself, but you didn't show?
You needed you and you weren't there

We have so much more potential
Than to become what we despise
And I'm not giving up on the possibility of compromise
At last, our paths will converge in time
And the dingy song playing on the radio:
Life is a paved road spotted with sink holes
And a backseat of caged birds
Singing, singing, singing
On our long way home

Have you ever felt alone?
If you choose the dark, I'll be your moon
You will close your eyes to me
As your gears begin shifting
And we are bathing
In the afterglow
And even when those whispers of the night find you in the day,
I see you like you've never felt pain

Have you ever seen a cloud kingdom rebound?
I know it's just as hard in heaven
And just as beautiful as you
As beautiful as you allow yourself to be

And in this moment we are infinite,
Aren't we?

*Something cosmic broke the day you left.*

*Our rose died before it could bloom, didn't it?*

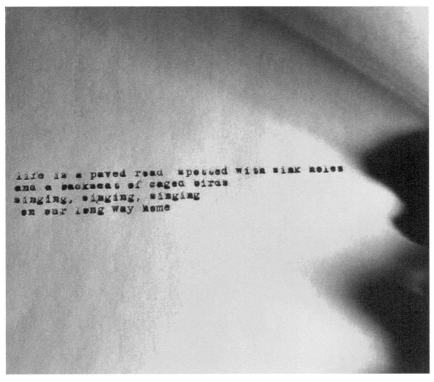

*Life is a paved road spotted with sink holes and a backseat of caged birds singing, singing, singing on our long way home.*

in this moment, we are infinite.

*In this moment, we are infinite.*

# Sister Feline

He found himself straying from his morals
And he spent his nights drinking candles
Her touch was so gentle
But her claws were not
Sister feline shone blue in the windowpane,
A spirit to unknot

His rickety soapbox upon which he stood
Talking about how he's tired of people
Not wanting people good
Through the angry shouts of the crowd,
Did he picture a squirming thing in a crib
Optimism and he had a waning relationship

And off to the stables he went wandering about
His eyes were estranged like a lone dog in the pound
And that dreadful stable boy spoke with his language so profound
And the boy sauntered out of sight with a casket of hate in his chest
His lungs did as they do: breathe to life things he thought died inside,
Talking about, "You hated me for the way people loved me
And now I can't even love myself"
And so he left the boy to chat with himself,
More than he did with anybody else

He wished to depart from his affairs with a cry from the wind
And he steered away from the house of the old bathtub gin
And the horses from the night he long buried his sins
And right past he dove from where he gathered the animal skins
So he long locked away the things that made every part of him

His rickety soapbox upon which he last
Talked about how we burn ourselves down
Until we learn to love the ash
Through the angry shouts of the crowd,

Did he picture the old rolling pins of his mother's shepherd's pie
Why is it that when we finally wake up,
The battle's won by those less than dignified?

He threw away the dingy sashes of the bedroom window
And he struggled with the creature who smells of clove
He dashed across the beds of dead tulips
Stashed in his pockets lies his mother's treasure trove

He wished to depart from his affairs with a cry from the wind
And he steered away from the house of the old bathtub gin
And the horses from the night he long buried his sins
And right past he dove from where he gathered the animal skins
So he long locked away the things that made every part of him

And he ran fast for his mother, he ran fast for his sin,
Ran for the world that was surely caving in
He ran fast for the stars, he ran fast for the stables,
Ran for every shard of glass his mother held
When he would ask of angels

He ran fast for the priests, he ran fast for the lines crossed,
He ran for every sky that beamed with the crisp December frost
He ran fast for the horses, he ran fast for every clothesline,
He ran for every child like his sister,
Whose eyes shone like a feline

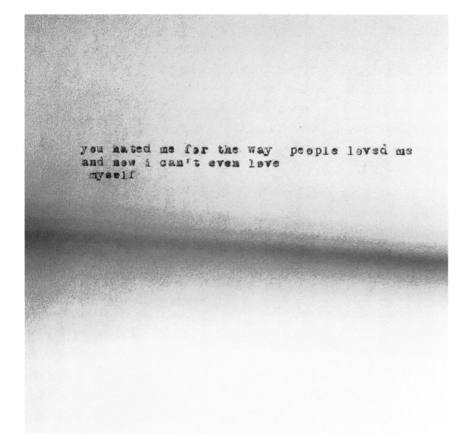

*You hated me for the way people loved me and now I can't even love myself.*

*We burn ourselves down until we learn to love the ash.*

# *chameleon*

She was my smile
The saddest one, she was my smile
"The world is not a nice place," she'd write,
"But there are nice things in the world.
And finding them, in itself, is a nice thing."
She was as constant as change;
A penny for your thoughts even on the brightest day
Kindness is strength to be forged,
And with her strength should she bloom green grasses
In the trenches of those mourned

Love is not a game;
You cannot make a game out of something it is not
But flowers do bloom side by side
And I'll spend my entire life, you see,
Forgiving myself for every petal that should wilt and die
And it's always the ones who save everyone else,
They are the ones who drown themselves
How maddening it must be
To stare tired eyes in the soul
And demand they draw their sword
When they couldn't care to be free

"But I deserve to feel freedom,
And not tremble in its wake," she'd write,
For she is none but an exhausted creature with no wings to fly—
And no desire to
I don't remember how it happened;
I just remember how it felt
When the cards we were dealt were placed on the table
And perhaps we're all just cabinets of wonders
Destined to keep our doors shut
To feel unsafe in freedom is an uncaged bird still scared to sing

But I unlocked your cage
And being free held no answers

And perhaps that's all we are:
Products of a system
Never meant to fall back together
Why are humans forced to breathe when living is so suffocating?
And I had called her reckless. And I was right.
How could she feel so alive in the presence
Of everything that could ever kill her?
She'd chain herself to the tree of her chosen fortune
And meet my eyes as if I gave her fever

"You're not afraid of being touched,
You're afraid of it being real," in my memory she'd scar.
But you are an entire galaxy.
And I, a single star.
And I wait for you
Yes, I wait for you
Yes, I wait for you in the fire
Every golden flame, every frantic ripple
And you'll be writing how you are so unimpressed
And you'll be writing the fire
Because we are the fire
We are the fire

"You could divert a river sooner than you could deny the pleasantries
of my nature.
If only there was enough time in the world."
That was the last thing she wrote.

*She was my smile. The saddest one, she was my smile.*

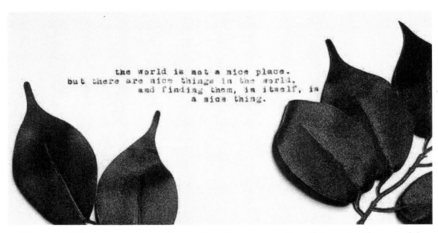

*The world is not a nice place. But there are nice things in the world. And finding them, in itself, is a nice thing.*

*But flowers do bloom side by side and I'll spend my entire life, you see,*
*forgiving myself for every flower that should wilt and die.*

*But flowers do bloom side by side and I'll spend my entire life, you see, forgiving myself for every flower that should wilt and die.*

*To feel unsafe in freedom is an uncaged bird still scared to sing.*

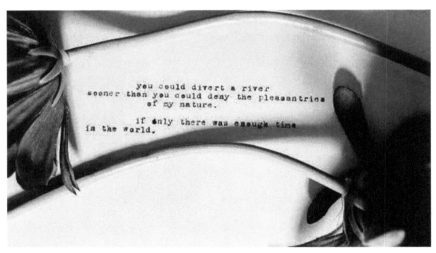

*You could divert a river sooner than you could deny the pleasantries of my nature. If only there was enough time in the world.*

# On the bayou

The house is creaking
You hope it falls down
You hope they scandalize their peers
And have to leave town
Hoping that old rain gets caught in their throats
While they're singing all the high notes
And you hope the corpse frowns as it drifts away

Those eyes pore over atrocities
I wonder how many you engineered
We can never get away from ourselves
But fate will meet you at the frontier
We'd walk home screaming
If emptiness did make sounds
But they'll never hear us
They'll never hear us now

You can't save everybody;
We are meant to save ourselves
You could pinch every penny
And still go fishing in the well
You could set on your journey
Before the sky spills into dawn
And still only be left to wonder
What truly lies beyond

I know of a life you never got to have
And I beat with you, with or without it
Your webs of scars
I draw like spiders
I can't promise it'll be beautiful
But I can promise you are

You sink into these waters that are written in your blood
A broken heart is a heart that's been loved
A wrinkled face is one that's smiled enough
And our fates are never painted with the same brush

And you sit and wait for me
But the sun never strikes my eyes
For I am tucked inside your chest
Whispering my stolen lullabies
And you smile now as you drift away,
Your face awash with shades of gray
And soon the sky should turn to another day
Another morning on the bayou

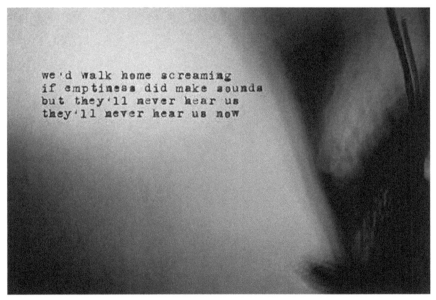

*We'd walk home screaming if emptiness did make sounds, but they'll never hear us, they'll never hear us now.*

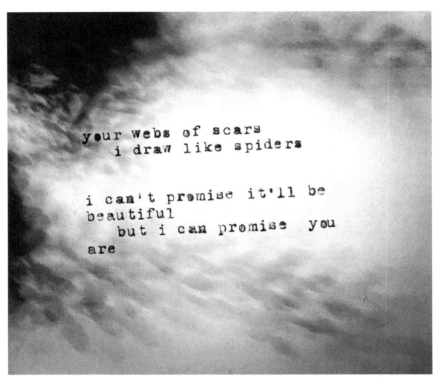

*Your webs of scars, I draw like spiders; I can't promise it'll be beautiful, but I can promise you are.*

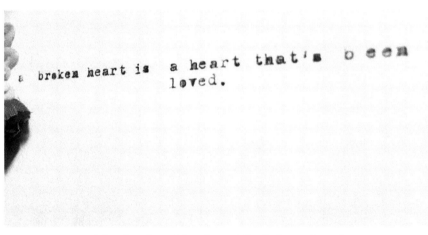

*A broken heart is a heart that's been loved.*

# *Know our names*

I'm afraid the days are stringing together, my love
I'm afraid of this hole in my chest
I'm afraid of every inch of myself
And when the sun's yolk blooms fire and spills into dawn
And we all carry on,
I'll still remember that look on your face

You dreamt of a garden of folklore
You watched as the waves nearly met the shore
The fish of these waters, they shone wounds that will never heal
Always grasping for more than they deserve
You must walk away before I leave you first
But we are products of a world that will never feel

And you held me how you did last night
And we sunk inside
For a little while as they wrote
All the promises they would break:
Every solution to every question,
Every fake smile void of redemption
And our eyes, they are as vacant as the world appears

But we patch ourselves together, reading between the lines
We steer into the sky as we're flying blind
We thought we lost all we could,
But there's always something left to lose
We are the children of old-world tinkerers
And we are out of time

We carry on as the days go by
We swallow the guilt like we swallow the food we refuse
And out flow the regrets like water of a dam that broke loose
But these waters we could never purify
And now I know that we never bleed to die

Zippers always did echo off these flimsy walls
I watch the web of cracks in that old savings jar
I flip off the light switch and the dark pours
This world was never ours, but at least I'm yours;
I'm sorry the world doesn't care to protect us,
But I will always protect you
We are born to run,
And so I run towards flame

We ended the way we started—
With fire
And your mind could warp every memory,
But you will know our names

*We are the children of old world tinkerers and we are out of time.*

*We ended the way we started—with fire.*

## Parental Guidance

Count the stars
That's how many sides of our story there are
To run so fast and never get far
Let's just call it a draw

Parents warn children of drugs in the streets,
But never the ones with emerald eyes
And that steady, steady heartbeat
Truthfully, I think I said goodbye a long time ago
Hard being tangled in someone who cares but it never shows
Used to think I could never go unloved by you;
I'm too knotted in your soul
Just how quickly the glass shatters when the winds of change blow

"Nothing will break us
not even ourselves"
Not the devil but you wore it well
All these lies you told me have tired
And now it's hardwired
In my brain to believe I never make sense
My mind is just a windy tunnel of unraveling descent
A meaningless stockpile of deficits
Worst part is knowing I can't refute
There's too much truth in a liar's words I can't refuse

When did deceit become a fashion trend?
Never knew selfishness was something that could be lent
You knew how well I mirrored the motions of you
Now I have you reflecting in the chains around my neck
You couldn't be saved in our spiraling train wreck
I wish you knew

We were but fickle-minded beings desperate for peace of mind
I fell too far into yours until I couldn't find mine

Your own shadow is never good company when you're yearning to feel alive
Breaking and healing is all the same when you must make the same sacrifice
Even when the wind blows you sideways, you make me into something I despise
Maybe I could love you if our stars had aligned
But now my only task is to leave you to fantasize

Count the stars
That's how many hearts you drove into the ground
But I promise the favor can be returned;
In fact, there is too much love to be burned
A broken heart is already in shards; you merely scattered the pieces
I no longer swim in the course of their bloodstream,
For now I have warned you of that steady, steady heartbeat

parents warn children of drugs in the streets
but never the ones with emerald eyes
and that steady, steady heartbeat
heartbeat

*Parents warn children of drugs in the streets but never ones with emerald eyes and that steady, steady heartbeat.*

*Nothing will break us, not even ourselves.*

*There's too much truth in a liar's words I can't refuse.*

```
your own shadow is never good  company
    when you're yearning to feel alive

            /

        breaking and healing is all the  same
    when you must make the same  sacrifice
```

*Your own shadow is never good company when you're yearning to feel alive; breaking and healing is all the same when you must make the same sacrifice.*

# *meg*

I had an old friend
She slept by bottles of alcohol
And nobody did question
Her drunken drawings on the walls
She left the town each day
She fished for quarters in the fountains
She needs the water to drown it

She would ride the bus singing
About how she should float away
She called it a modern saving grace
She'd walk the chalk right off the sidewalks
And befriend the town's white moths
Adorned with jewels they slyly contemplate

Green was the color of her bedroom as she wiped the slate white
Her thoughts lie nestled in her curly hair
Always shadowed by the soft arc light
And her height did soar above the rafters
Neighbors kept her from the children
But the pigeons were convinced her crown
Was the highest heaven

She'd wake in her makings of homemade lace in the warm mornings
And the cat did paw her like she pawed the spiders in the lawns
Of the farmstead
Should she take this as one of mother nature's warnings
That she should finally get out of bed

When people lean in, she gets mad when they fall
As her body leans on the park bench, her mind inside the world she
built herself,
She wishes she could lie as easily as she could leave
But the shards of this mirror belong to nobody else

Whether you're running away
Or running towards something,
She is not your destination
But she's right here now
And I hope she stays

And should she store the pens in the old ice box tonight,
So her ink never dries out
So my ink never dries out

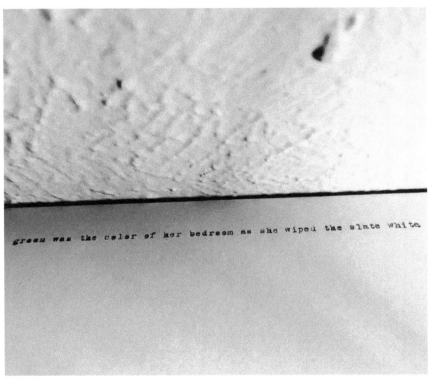

*Green was the color of her bedroom as she wiped the slate white.*

*Whether you're running away or running towards something, she is not your destination.*

# *inkwells*

I know positivity is your rival
I know you're existing in your denial
You weep into the tear vial spacebar You're begging for your survival
You resent all of your deprival
I know you wish for your reprisal
Tried to cure this infection with an antiviral
Well, I say welcome to your revival

Life is just a cycle of giving and receiving, commodities or all your
feelings
It is forever repeating, scarred with memories of deceiving
Perpetually overwhelmed, trying to find a better version of yourself
To breathe love, you have to give some air to somebody else

I know you push yourself to look at the benefits
Then guilt-trip your mind for overstepping the lines; you could never be
delicate
Hard to make it through these times when you stop to reminisce
Isn't staying motivated a skill so easily dismissed?

Waste away thinking you had never tried
How easily you make yourself believe you live life just to get by
I know you feel more than you show on the outside
But loving is part of humans' design
I know you battle with the advice
Just want to draw a smile on and wallow in the disguise
Can't bother to comply with the feelings you fail to describe
The chalk in the driveway, we'll redraw this outline
Your terror of freedom leaves you still in these confines
Let's take a deep breath, I promise the world has enough time

Your body thinks it's doing what you want it to do
You feed it thinking you deserve what you go through
But you can repaint these lines that you never drew

You can recycle the energy you use to break down and refuse
And transmit it into love, a passion to pursue
Your flowers were cut too early and naturally you withdrew
But your roots, you had forgotten they are designed to refute

The key is to not find a side you love
But to love every side
We have to make these years count
Why live just to die?

To live cautiously, you recede
You have willingly chosen to use up all your air to breathe
Encase yourself in the false uncertainty
Overthink the holes in your apologies
The heart doesn't have to be full to be loved
I just wish you understood you are a thousand times enough

To think that love is all around you
How come you feel distant?
You spit all of your problems
How come no one ever listens?

Got you sitting here writing letters
You can't release the addiction
Too wounded with this lack of validation
Wonder what people gain from following your misdirection

And you lied to yourself again
You don't know what it's like
Driving a car instead of the edge of this temptingly sharp knife
I'll teach you how to dig yourself out of the hole
To believe that you're all right, without it feeling like a lie
Or sinking back into your disguise; instability is not an alibi

And now you will prove your strength
By accepting your own apology

Apologizing to your mirror for what it's seen
And to your mind for encouraging
The pure gloaming that kept you from
All the beautiful outcomes
That you gift yourself the time
To experience with your own two eyes

But it's hard to shut it off, almost unthinkable to make it stop
And I catch a burst of doubt with its lack of open mouth:
"We're just small, undetectable pieces
In this whole wide world
So tell me, once it's over,
What will we become?"

I drain myself inside these inkwells
We will overcome

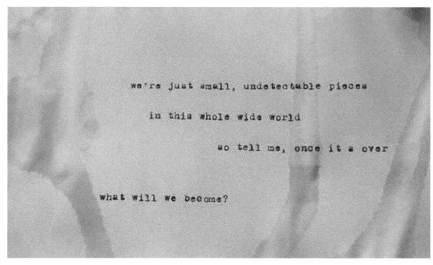

*We're just small, undetectable pieces in this whole wide world, so tell me, once it's over, what will we become?*

*I drain myself inside these inkwells; we will overcome.*

*Mom (bonus piece)*

Dear treasured reader,

I've always had the extraordinary ability to choke on my words. Stuttering, accidentally spitting on my peers, deciding it's best to just smile and nod, the like. Even now, typing this, I'm struggling with how to word this little author's note, or whatever you'd like to call it. First thing's first, though, the piece I am about to introduce you to was gifted to my mother for Mother's Day 2019. The exact reason of its significance is quite unknown even to myself, but I do have a couple ideas. This is one of the fastest pieces I've ever written, not just because of its small length compared to my other pieces, but the fact that the words were simply rolling off my tongue. I had no trouble constructing the sentences, the ideas, my *mother*. I had no trouble constructing my best friend (even though this poem does her absolutely no justice). And from someone who is horribly obsessive and likes to take their time to tinker (that's the best way I can word it), telling someone that you wrote a poem for them in less than five minutes flat is a tremendous compliment.

I had a point to this, I promise: I'd like to take the time to personally thank my mother for her dedication to my wellbeing, mentally and physically. You sat beside me on the floor of my bedroom on the nights I'd sob from the stomach pains because I'd refuse to let myself eat; you'd respond to every letter I hastily shoved under your office door because I couldn't articulate my feelings verbally; and, probably against your better judgement, you let me hibernate in my room for all those months (aside from the occasional grocery store run). You've shown me strength, you've shown me pain, and you've shown me just how loudly you can play the piano so I can hear it from my room to calm my anxiety. Mom, I love you, and everything you are.

Secondly, of course, I love and appreciate all the space and time I was granted to heal, from my father and my brother, while I graciously latched on to my mother for dear life (much to her comfort, I'm sure). The restrictions I've placed on myself have hindered our relationships, I know, but I also know that *you* know that I love you and I'd do absolutely everything in my power to keep you all well and safe.

And above all, I hope each and every being on all nine planets has been blessed with even just a single person, with even just a single glimpse of what my mother holds. And, if you believe you have not, I'll be yours. Always.

Finally, a message to everyone struggling with mental health or circumstance: "We will overcome."

## *Mom (bonus piece)*

i don't want to be immune to life's afflictions,
but find the peace within them.

i don't want to be trembling in life's adversities,
but be cradled in their allusiveness.

i don't want to shatter in life's desolation,
but persist in the broken shards.

i want to be just like you.

happy mother's day.

*feeling suicidal?*

National Suicide Prevention Hotline: 1-800-273-8255
National Mental Illness Hotline: 1-800-950-6264
Dating Abuse and Domestic Violence Hotline: 1-866-331-9474
Sexual Assault Hotline: 1-800-656-4673
National Eating Disorder Hotline: 1-800-931-2237
Bullying Hotline: 1-800-420-1479
Transgender Suicide Hotline: 877-565-8860
The Trevor Project (suicide hotline for LGBTQIA+ youths): 866-488-7386
Self-Harm Hotline: 1-800-DONT-CUT / 1-800-344-HELP
Runaway Hotline: 1-800-843-5200 / 1-800-843-5678
Depression Hotline: 1-630-482-9696
General Crisis Text Line: Text SUPPORT to 741-741
Abuse Hotline: 1-800-799-7233 / 1-800-787-3224
Addiction Hotline: 800-910-3734
Exhale (post-abortion hotline/pro-voice): 1-866-439-4235
Poison Control: 1-800-222-1222

Giving to other people helps me feel better. If you would like to:

Text ENOUGH / FLOYD to 55156 to sign a Color of Change petition
Text JUSTICE to 668366 to sign a MoveOn petition
Sign a petition at JusticeForBigFloyd
Donate to the Black Lives Matter Movement
Volunteer or apply for an internship with the National Alliance on Mental Illness (NAMI)
Volunteer and donate to the Trevor Project
Donate to the Human Rights Campaign
Donate to UNICEF
Donate to the ASPCA
Donate to support Lebanon's aid
Support Nigeria and *End SARS*, a movement against police brutality in Nigeria

Lightning Source UK Ltd.
Milton Keynes UK
UKHW051002110722
405669UK00002B/8